DYING OF EMBARRASSMENT

Help for Social Anxiety & Phobia

BARBARA G. MARKWAY, Ph.D.
CHERYL N. CARMIN, Ph.D.
C. ALEC POLLARD, Ph.D.
TERESA FLYNN, Ph.D.

NEW HARBINGER PUBLICATIONS, INC.

Publisher's Note

This publication is designed to provide accurate and authoritative information in regard to the subject matter covered. It is sold with the understanding that the publisher is not engaged in rendering psychological, financial, legal, or other professional services. If expert assistance or counseling is needed, the services of a competent professional should be sought.

Distributed in the U.S.A. by Publishers Group West; in Canada by Raincoast Books; in Great Britain by Airlift Book Company, Ltd.; in South Africa by Real Books, Ltd.; in Australia by Boobook; and in New Zealand by Tandem Press.

Library of Congress Catalog Number: 92-061814
ISBN 1-879237-23-7 Paperback
ISBN 1-879237-24-5 Hardcover

Printed in the United States of America on recycled paper.

Cover: SHELBY DESIGNS & ILLUSTRATES; illustration: Phil Cheung

02   01   00

20   19   18   17   16   15   14   13

Contents

Acknowledgments

As with any project of this magnitude, we have many people to thank. First and foremost, we acknowledge the contributions of the individuals with social phobia we have treated over the years. It was out of their need that this book was inspired. They have taught us much about the effect of social phobia on their lives and how treatment can provide hope and enable them to overcome their fears.

We would also like to thank Ronald B. Margolis, Ph.D., Director of the Division of Behavioral Medicine at St. Louis University Medical Center, for his support in this undertaking. In addition, our appreciation goes to the other psychologists at the Anxiety Disorders Center who over the years have contributed their ideas on the treatment of social phobia. We also recognize with gratitude Maureen Aichs, who did the word processing on the early drafts of many of the chapters. Her patience and sense of humor in the face of impossible deadlines was greatly appreciated. We also thank Mary Guy and Stephanie Stemmler for their help.

Several of our physician colleagues took the time to review the chapter on medication. The thoughtful input of Tracy Ware, M.D.; S. Terry Moore, D.O.; Sue Perrine, M.D.; and Shael Bronson, M.D. helped to insure that the information contained in this chapter was both accurate and reflective of the current pharmacologic treatment of social phobia. Two of our other colleagues, Greg Markway, Ph.D., and Heidi Pollard, M.S.N., C.S., reviewed countless revisions of the other chapters and offered valuable suggestions each step of the way. Their contributions are much appreciated.

Many thanks to Barbara Quick for her skillful editing. She was a pleasure to work with and made the entire editing process as painless as possible. We also thank Patrick Fanning for his cooperation at key points in the process.

Last, but certainly not least, we would like to thank our family members and significant others. They provided us with support and encouragement, shared in our enthusiasm, and picked up the slack at home when we were busy writing.

Introduction

Literally millions of people suffer from social phobia, a problem that can interfere considerably with your satisfaction and enjoyment of life. Despite the prevalence and potential severity of social phobia, finding help for this problem can be very difficult. In certain areas of the country, there are no qualified professionals with the needed expertise. Even in large cities, only a handful of mental health professionals are well versed in the treatment of social phobia. Most of what is known about the disorder and its treatment has been discovered in recent years. Thus, a primary goal of the authors in writing this book is to bring this information directly to people with a social phobia. Many of you will be able to overcome your social anxiety successfully on your own by following the program outlined in the book. Others will decide to use the book as an adjunct to therapy with a professional.

We have also written this book for friends and relatives of people with social phobia. They, too, can benefit from learning more about this anxiety disorder, so that they are better able to understand and help the socially fearful person.

Finally, we also hope to spread the word about our treatment methods to other mental health professionals. Many of our colleagues in the field may be interested in this topic, but are relatively inexperienced in treating social phobias. Although much of the information presented here could also be obtained by poring over professional journals and texts, many clinicians may value its availability in one easy-to-use source.

Thus, we recognize that people who read this book will have somewhat different problems and needs. At the same time, we want each reader to obtain the maximum benefit possible. With these things in mind, we suggest the following approach to using *Dying of Embarrassment*. Section I contains essential information that should be helpful to virtually anyone with social fears. The chapters in this section are important for obtaining a basic understanding of social phobia and how you might be affected by it. The chapters in Section II will assist you in setting your goals and objectives for recovery, assessing your fears, and developing a personalized recovery plan. Next, Section III offers important coping skills to handle your physical and mental reactions to fear, while Section IV is designed to help you confront and overcome your fears through a procedure called "exposure." Section V may be one that you choose to use selectively. Based on your needs and your progress with recovery, you may wish to read further about one or more of the following topics in this section: social skills, stress management, incentives, coexisting problems, relapse prevention, medication, and professional help. Finally, we offer some speculations about the direction that scientific research on social phobia might take in the near future.

One more note on how to use *Dying of Embarrassment*. This book is meant to be one that you use actively. Simply reading the book may be of some benefit. However, to reap the full rewards of this treatment approach, you will need to follow the methods described and complete the exercises in the book as you go. We've provided space to write in each chapter, so you can use the text as a workbook.

We, the authors, wish you the best of luck in making use of this book. Based on our experiences with people seeking help for social anxiety, we are optimistic that you can become more comfortable in social situations than you ever thought possible!

SECTION I

Understanding Social Phobias: The Fear of Disapproval

In these chapters, you will find basic information about social phobia. The disorder is defined in Chapter 1, and various examples of it are provided. In Chapter 2, you will learn about current theories and research about the roots of social anxiety.

1

The Nature of Social Phobia

What Is Social Phobia?

Social phobia is a *disorder* characterized by a persistent fear of criticism or rejection by others. People with social phobias fear they may behave in a way that will be embarrassing or humiliating. Take George, for example. He has a social phobia. He is so afraid of making a mistake in front of co-workers that he frequently stays late to finish his work after others have gone home. His anticipation of being judged as incompetent or stupid is so frightening for George that he tries to avoid situations where there is any potential for embarrassment.

Social phobia is also a psychiatric *diagnosis*. You may be thinking to yourself, "What's the difference? Disorder? Diagnosis? Aren't they the same thing?" The answer is no. The disorder is what you actually feel and experience. The diagnosis is a label, which mental health professionals use to identify the disorder from its signs and symptoms.

"What's the point?" you may ask. The point is that social phobia has only been listed as a diagnostic category in the *Diagnostic and Statistical Manual of Mental Disorders* (called *DSM*) since 1980. The *DSM* is the guide most frequently used in the United States for making psychiatric diagnostic decisions. It lists and describes all the major mental health problems that are currently recognized as such by a panel of experts. In 1987, the criteria for social phobia, or rules for making the diagnosis, were revised with the publication of *DSM-III-R*, which is the name of the current edition.

"How can this be? I had this problem long before 1980!" That's right. Many of you have suffered with social anxiety since you were children. What is important for you to realize is that social phobia as a diagnostic category has only recently come to the attention of mental health professionals, and our understanding of this disorder is changing at a rapid rate. Even now as we are writing, work is being done to prepare for the publication of the next revised edition of the diagnostic manual, *DSM-IV*.

This historical background may help put things in perspective for you. It did for 35-year-old Renée, who has experienced disabling social anxiety since her adolescence. She frequently blamed herself for not seeking professional help for her problems many years earlier. However, Renée now realizes that she would have had a very difficult time finding a professional who could understand her social fears, much less how to treat them.

Although *DSM-III-R* is probably not the last word on social phobia, for the time being it is what we will work from. The definition reads as follows:

> *Social phobia is a persistent fear of one or more situations in which the person is exposed to possible scrutiny by others and fears that he or she may do something or act in a way that will be humiliating or embarrassing.*

In essence, social phobia is a fear of the disapproval of others. Although it's natural to be concerned about whether others approve of you, individuals with social phobia take this concern to an extreme. As you'll see in the next section, fearing disapproval can make even everyday situations unbearable.

Common Situations in Which Social Fears Occur

There are many situations in which social fears can crop up, but several are particularly common:

- Public speaking
- Entertaining an audience
- Taking tests
- Eating in restaurants
- Writing in public
- Using public restrooms
- Dating

When people become afraid of one of these situations they are said to have a specific social phobia. Specific social phobias involve a focused area of fear, discomfort, and avoidance. People with this kind of social phobia dread one or a limited number of particular situations, although they may be relatively comfortable in other social settings. Specific social phobias usually involve *performance anxiety*—concern that some task or behavior will be executed in an incorrect or unacceptable way. Let's look at the most common situations in which social phobias develop.

Public Speaking

Public speaking is consistently ranked as the most frequently feared social situation in the United States. If you are terrified to speak to a group of people, you may have this type of specific social phobia. Fear of public speaking can seriously interfere with your life. This was certainly the case for José, a 38-year-old salesperson. He did fine making the sale when it was a one-on-one presentation. However, if he had to give a sales pitch to a group of people, he was in trouble. Speaking even to a gathering of three people was sure to make him extremely nervous. He complained of sweating, rapid heart rate, and shortness of breath. He was sure others would notice that there was something wrong with him. He worried that he would sound stupid and that people would think that he didn't know his product line. José even worried that someone would report him to his supervisor as being incompetent. He tried to avoid these group sales presentations whenever possible. José was trying to save up for his children's college education and was sure he'd lost a lot of money because of his fear of public speaking.

If you are one of the many with this particular fear, your worries may be very similar to José's. You may have additional concerns as well, which may sound something like this: "What if others notice I'm anxious?"; "What if they can see my hands trembling?"; "What if I stumble on my words?"; "Worse yet, what if I totally forget what I'm supposed to say?"; "What if someone asks me a question I can't answer?"; "What if I sound stupid?"; "What if my voice quivers?" You can probably add several other anxieties to this list.

Entertaining an Audience

Commonly referred to as "stagefright," entertaining an audience is another social situation that is often feared. If you have this phobia, you may be able to perform a task requiring great skill, as long as you are alone. However, performing in front of others—well, that's another matter!

This type of phobia is common even among professional athletes. For example, Los Angeles Dodger second baseman, Steve Sax, was named Rookie-of-the-Year in 1982. However, during the following season he suddenly found it difficult to make even routine throws to first base. More recently, New York Mets catcher Mackey Sasser developed a problem with throwing the ball back to the pitcher—something that most catchers never even think about. What do you think could have happened to cause such a drastic turnaround in these players' performance? Sax had made a few bad throws early in the season and became increasingly focused on not making another mistake. The more he concentrated on not making another bad throw, the more anxious he became. The more anxious he became, the worse he actually performed. The situation was similar for Sasser.

Taking Tests and Writing

Two common terms, *test anxiety* and *writer's block*, actually refer to the social fears of taking tests and writing. A bright seventh-grader, Anne, experienced both of these. She studied hard, but her grades were only average. Anne didn't think it was fair that she could work so hard and get only C's. The typical scenario for Anne went something like this. The night before she had an exam, her mother quizzed her on the material, which Anne almost always knew well. However, the morning of the test, Anne woke up feeling nervous. She worried that she might not know the material well enough or that her mind would go blank, which had happened in the past. Despite her mother's reassurance, Anne became so tense that she could barely eat any breakfast. Sometimes she was even in tears before she got to school. When she sat down to actually take the test, she couldn't concentrate. The words looked blurry to her and she noticed her heart beating rapidly. In fulfillment of her worst fear, she felt her mind go completely blank.

One of Anne's teachers required her students to write essays in class. This presented another problem situation for Anne. Although she could write fluently at home, her ideas came to a standstill under the pressure of writing in class.

You don't have to be a student to experience writer's block. It's quite common for people whose job depends on writing—for example, journalists—to experience writer's block from time to time. The common fear is that whatever you produce, whether it's test answers or a newspaper article, will be inadequate and unacceptable to others.

Eating in Restaurants

Eating anyplace where others might be watching is yet another specific situation in which social phobias can develop. If you have this fear, you may worry that you will do something embarrassing, such as spill your drink all over yourself or your companions. You may also have a vague sense that others are watching you, which makes you feel even clumsier with your food. These kinds of worries often become self-fulfilling prophecies. The more you worry about the possibility of doing something embarrassing, the more anxious you become. The more anxious you become, the more likely you are to actually begin trembling or make abrupt, clumsy movements. This problem can build to the point where it becomes difficult to get food or a beverage to your mouth without dropping or spilling it.

This was the situation for Angela. She was close to her family and wanted to be a part of family celebrations and get-togethers. And yet the family gatherings had become unbearable ordeals for her. She began to shake when the family assembled around the table. Angela tried to hide her anxiety; but the more she tried to hide it, the worse it got. She became a master at scooting her food around on the plate to make it look as if she was eating. When she got home from one of these family functions, she was famished. Much to her confusion, she had no difficulty eating in the privacy of her own home.

Writing in Public

Writing in public is another situation that can cause a great deal of anxiety for people. Imagine being unable to sign your name in front of a sales clerk! Imagine not being able to take out a loan because you would be unable to get through all of the signatures and paperwork required! If you have this type of phobia, your concerns may have evolved something like this. At one point, you may have worried that your handwriting was sloppy. Or perhaps you were sensitive about the possibility of misspelling a word, or that your hand would shake as you wrote. Whatever the case, your worries escalated to the point where your hand may have actually become a little shaky and you did, in fact, have difficulty writing. Your handwriting may be beautiful as long as no one is watching you. Or you may have become so sensitive, that even if no one else is around, just the thought that someone may see your handwriting is enough to make you worry.

Doreen, a 20-year-old education major, had this phobia. She was doing her student teaching at a local junior high school. She had always been a little self-conscious about her handwriting; now she was worried about having to write on the blackboard. What if her new students noticed she was nervous? What if her arm shook? What if the students didn't take her seriously because of her poor writing? Doreen did everything she could to avoid writing on the board. She stayed up until late at night planning every detail of her lessons for the next day. She went to school early every morning to make copies of typed handouts and assignments, arriving at her classroom with armloads of materials.

Using Public Restrooms

Another social phobia is the fear of using public restrooms. If you have this problem, you may have been too embarrassed to tell anyone about it.

This was the case for Amy, who had never told anyone that she had enormous anxieties about using public restrooms. She could go into the toilet stall, but if anyone else was in the restroom, her muscles became so tense that she was unable to urinate. Amy wondered if something was wrong with her. Maybe she was crazy. Maybe she had a physical problem. Finally, when Amy went for a yearly routine physical, she resolved to tell her physician about her problem urinating. She felt terribly anxious about broaching the subject—what if the doctor laughed at her? She worried about this for days prior to the examination.

When Amy presented her problem, the doctor assured her that it was unlikely to have a physical origin: she just had a "bashful bladder." The technical name for this problem is "psychogenic urinary retention." Amy felt somewhat relieved to have a name for it. But what was she to do about it? She was quite active with volunteer work, and it was becoming more and more difficult to plan breaks in her schedule so she could go home to use the bathroom.

Fear of using public restrooms is one fear that may present itself somewhat differently in men and women, largely due to the differences in the way men's and women's public restrooms are set up. If you are a woman with this phobia, you may worry that you have to hurry to urinate, especially if there is a line of people waiting. For Amy, busy airport restrooms were the worst. She worried that she would take too long and that the other women would become angry. She also worried what others might think of her. "Why is she taking so long?" "What could she possibly be doing in there?" In addition, some people may also be sensitive to the sounds they make. Although Amy knew that everyone urinates and that everyone makes noise, this still bothered her. It always helped her if a fan was on to block out the other sounds. Some people with this type of phobia also worry about passing gas ("farting") or defecating in a public restroom.

If you are a man with this phobia, your fears are likely to take on a slightly different form due to the fact that most men's restrooms do not have private stalls for urinating. Dave had this particular problem. If other men were around when he went to use a urinal, he became anxious that he would not be able to urinate right away. As he stood there, waiting to urinate, his thoughts would run wild. "What if the other men think I'm some kind of pervert?" "They might think I'm masturbating because I'm taking so long." "What if they think I'm gay?" In fact, his anxiety made things worse by making it even more difficult for him to urinate.

Dating

Dating is another situation that provokes social fears. You may be able to speak to a group of 100 people with little anxiety, and yet be terrified at the prospect of going out on a date. Take Michael, for example. As a new college professor, he frequently gave lectures to large groups of students. During his free time, he enjoyed going to movies and sporting events with several male friends. Despite Michael's ease in most social situations, he was fearful of asking a woman out for a date. He was afraid that she'd say no, and of his subsequent feeling of rejection. He was also afraid that she might say yes—once on a date, Michael worried that he would do something to embarrass himself. Consequently, he didn't date.

Although some social anxiety is common on dates, a dating phobia can be quite debilitating, sometimes preventing people from having any intimate relationships.

Some sexual dysfunctions can be a form of social phobia and can also wreak havoc with relationships. Bruce, for example, a medical school student in his early twenties, was very unsure of himself when it came to women, even though women found him attractive. Bruce had one girlfriend during his senior year of college. He thought everything was going well, until their relationship moved in a more intimate direction. He was so anxious about whether or not he would be able to perform sexually that he was unable to achieve an erection when he was with his girlfriend. However, he was perfectly capable of getting an erection when alone. When Bruce moved away to attend medical school, he and his girlfriend broke up. Now he is reluctant to develop another relationship, for fear that the pattern will repeat itself.

When You're Afraid of Many (or All) Social Situations

In contrast to people with specific social phobias, you may dread many, if not all, situations in which there is a chance of experiencing disapproval. People with these widespread social fears are said to have a *generalized* social phobia. In addition to fearing a variety of social situations, people with generalized social phobias are also more likely to lack certain skills, such as how to be assertive or how to communicate effectively, that are important ingredients for feeling comfortable with other people. As you'll see below in the case of Rebecca, having a generalized social phobia can be extremely pervasive and debilitating, affecting virtually every area of your life.

Rebecca was always a quiet child. She never spoke up in class, and dreaded the inevitable times when teachers would call on her to answer a question. She was teased by the other children for being so quiet and mouse-like. Despite her discomfort, Rebecca managed to get by until she reached college. No, she was never involved in any extracurricular activities. No, she never dated. And, no, she didn't have many friends. But, according to Rebecca, this time in her life was easy compared to what lay ahead.

Rebecca decided to go to a community college. Although she was bright, she didn't make very good grades in high school; community college seemed her only option. The year got off to a bad start. Rebecca came down with mononucleosis. She had to miss a month of school and fell behind in her work. As if that weren't enough to deal with, Rebecca was still weak when she first began attending classes, and her hands were a bit unsteady and shaky. By now you've probably learned enough to guess what happened next. Rebecca started worrying that others would notice her hands trembling. Well, to make a long story short, Rebecca became paralyzed with fear, and was unable to keep her grades up. She soon dropped out of college.

Things went from bad to worse. Rebecca got a job working at a children's home. She was mostly to do paperwork, which she didn't mind too much, because she could work by herself. However, she was also supposed to assist at mealtimes, making sure that the children ate and behaved properly. Although Rebecca liked children, this part of the job was terrifying for her. When some of the children misbehaved, she was unable to deal with the situation. She was afraid to say anything. She soon quit this job. In fact, Rebecca tried out several different jobs, but ended up quitting, or getting fired from, each position.

Rebecca gave up on working and spent up to half of her day in bed. She felt it was the only place she could be safe from the scrutiny and evaluation of other people. When she was dressed and moving about her house, she worried that the phone might ring at any minute or that someone would knock at her door. Rebecca felt terribly guilty about her behavior. Here she was home all day long while her parents were away at work. She wished she could at least go to the grocery store so she could have dinner ready in the evening. Even what seemed to be everyday situations involving other people (such as handing the cashier her money) had become overwhelming for Rebecca. Although her parents tried to be understanding, they wished their daughter would try to get another job, maybe find a little apartment for herself, and find a nice young man to date. Sometimes they became so frustrated that they said things to Rebecca that they later regretted.

If you find yourself in a similar situation to Rebecca's, dreading almost all social contact, don't despair. Although overcoming a generalized social phobia of this magnitude will take time and hard work, it can be done. Following the guidelines outlined in the subsequent chapters of this book may be of great value to you. However, you may also find that you need to work with a trained mental health professional as well. We'll discuss when and how to find an appropriate therapist in Chapter 17.

What Are the Symptoms of Social Phobia?

The symptoms of social phobia can generally be grouped into three major categories. The first category includes the bodily symptoms of anxiety, which you experience when you are in, or when you are anticipating, the social situations you fear. The second category includes your cognitions (thoughts) and expectations about these social situations. The third category includes your actions or behaviors related to these situations. Let's go over the bodily symptoms first.

Bodily Symptoms

You are likely to experience a number of unpleasant bodily reactions when you fear social disapproval. These may include any one or combination of the following symptoms:

- Rapid heart rate, or heart palpitations
- Trembling or shaking
- Shortness of breath
- Sweating
- Blushing
- Abdominal distress
- Dizziness

You may also experience several other bodily symptoms. We'll help you assess your body's reaction to fear in Chapter 4, and teach you how to cope with these reactions in Chapter 5.

Sometimes these symptoms come on rapidly, become quite intense, and then diminish with time. This experience is called a *panic attack*. Panic is an apt word to describe the intense fear you may feel when confronted with certain social situations. In addition to these intense, panic-like experiences, you may also experience chronic tension from continually being "on your guard" around others. This chronic tension may result in headaches, fatigue, stomachaches, and other stress-related symptoms. Chapter 12 offers some tips on managing stress more effectively.

Cognitive Symptoms

In addition to experiencing a number of bodily symptoms of anxiety, you are likely to have certain thoughts about what you *should* be like in social situations. Notice that the word "should" is emphasized. Before you've finished working your way through this book, you'll learn that certain *should* words can be dangerous to your mental health!

When you're in a social situation and experiencing intense anxiety, you probably have a number of thoughts running through your mind. You may have these thoughts so often that they feel quite automatic, almost beyond your control. Imagine yourself in the last social situation that caused you anxiety. What kinds of thoughts were going through your mind? If you don't remember, that's okay. Often these thoughts are so quick that you may not be able to keep track of them at first. Some examples of the kinds of thoughts you may have include:

- *I look out of place.*

- *I sound stupid.*

- *I don't fit in.*

- *I'm blowing it.*

Many psychologists call these kinds of thoughts *irrational*. "Irrational" is defined in Webster's dictionary as "not based on reason" or "defective in mental power." Well, we don't think you're either defective in mental power or unreasonable. Rather, we prefer to label these thoughts as *maladaptive*. "Maladaptive" is defined as "poorly suited to a particular use, purpose, or situation." In other words, thinking this way does not serve you well in social situations. In fact, such thinking makes it much more likely that you'll become anxious and, as a consequence, perform poorly or uncomfortably. This is one of the most paradoxical features of anxiety—by thinking that the worst will happen, you may unwittingly bring this about. We'll help you assess the cognitive symptoms of your social phobia in Chapter 4. Chapter 6 will show you ways to challenge and ultimately change these unhealthy thinking patterns.

Behavioral Symptoms

The behavioral symptoms of social phobia are a response to your experience of intense discomfort in social situations. Like physical pain, anxiety is a warning signal that you need to take action. However, for people with social phobias, common responses to this warning signal are typically unhelpful.

The first of these responses—freezing—may not seem properly classifiable as an action at all. In fact, it's the absence of action. Freezing (or the more technical term, *atonic immobility*) is a largely involuntary, physiological response that can occur when you perceive danger. Initially, this response served to help our species evolve and survive, although currently it is largely maladaptive. In prehistoric times, the freezing response typically occurred in times of mortal danger, such as in the presence of a threatening animal. The freezing response provided time to assess the danger of the situation, and prevented impulsive actions that might provoke an attack. Immobility also provided the greatest chance of camouflage in cases where escape or aggression was impossible.

When human beings experience this freezing response, it inhibits or prevents voluntary actions, such as movement, speech, or recall. That's why when you are scared in a situation involving other people, you may be literally unable to talk. You might even find it difficult to remember your name or phone number! In essence, you feel paralyzed. What's important to remember is that this response is usually of very brief duration, and will pass if you remain in the situation a little longer.

Another behavioral symptom you're likely to experience is avoidance. We have already noted that because many social situations are uncomfortable for you, you are likely to avoid them altogether. Your avoidance is not unlike that of the person who is afraid of elevators and consequently chooses to take the stairs. However, not everyone avoids feared situations completely. Some people are unable or unwilling to avoid, and will suffer through, some of the situations they dread. Even they, however, may engage in subtle forms of avoidance. For example, you may enter a situation but then leave too soon. This is called *escape behavior*. Or, while in a social situation, you may attempt to distract yourself from acknowledging your surroundings: for example, your mind may wander, or you may fidget with a pen in your hand. You may also disengage yourself from the situation, perhaps by staring off into the corner, or somehow going into your own private world. Daydreaming is a common way in which people disengage. Both distraction and disengagement are forms of avoidance.

The importance of conquering these more subtle types of avoidance will become clear when you begin working your way through the chapters on treatment in Section IV. We will also try to show you how avoidance of any kind can make things worse for you in the long run.

How Common Is Social Phobia, and Whom Does It Affect?

Social phobia is quite common. It is the second most common anxiety disorder, and significantly impairs the lives of 2-to-3 percent of the population of the United States. An additional 20 percent have less distressing forms of social phobia because they are able to avoid the situation they dread. What this means is that literally millions of people suffer from social phobia. You are not alone!

"If social phobia is so common," you may ask, "why haven't I heard about it before?" That's a good question. One reason is that, unlike some other anxiety disorders, social phobia has received very little attention in the media. One group of experts has called social phobia the "neglected" anxiety disorder. Despite the diagnosis of social phobia being a relatively recent occurrence, the disorder itself dates back to ancient history. The ancient Greek, Hippocrates, considered to be the father of modern medicine, was described as having many of the characteristics of social phobia. Today such celebrities as Willard Scott and Carly Simon have openly discussed their struggle with social phobias.

Research has shown that social phobia seems to affect slightly more women than men in the general population. Traditionally, and especially in Victorian times, timidity has been considered a positive trait in women. In many nineteenth century novels, such words as "shy" and "retiring" are used as complimentary descriptions for women characters! It's not difficult to see how this tradition may have evolved into the greater prevalence of social phobias among women today. Social phobia is nonetheless common in both sexes, although men seem to be more likely than women to seek treatment. Although the reasons for this are unclear, it may be that social phobias interfere more with the types of jobs that still tend to be held predominantly by men. This may change as the roles of men and women continue to shift in our society.

The onset of social phobia is typically between the ages of 15 and 20, although it can begin at other times as well. You may remember feeling nervous about giving reports or talking in front of the class as early as elementary school. Current thinking about childhood anxiety disorders suggests that some school phobias (when children refuse to go to school because of fear) may be an early form of social phobia.

Until now, you may not have known that you have social phobia. Like Amy who was unable to urinate in public restrooms, you may have kept your problem hidden. You may have thought of yourself as freakishly afflicted, never imagining that your fears are in fact quite common. If you did gather the courage to tell someone else about your problem, you may have been met with well-meaning but trivializing comments such as, "Big deal! Everyone is nervous getting up in front of a crowd." Mental health professionals may not have had the slightest idea how to treat your problem.

Fortunately, much of this is changing. Many researchers have become interested in social phobias, and new treatments are being studied. The methods in this book have already proven to be very effective in helping many people overcome their social fears and anxiety. Help is available!

Summary

The essential feature of social phobia is a persistent fear of one or more situations in which you or your behavior may be evaluated by others; it is, in essence, a fear of disapproval. There are two types of social phobias. Specific social phobias involve a focused area of fear, discomfort, and avoidance. Common social situations around which a phobia can develop include public speaking, entertaining an audience, eating in restaurants, writing in public, taking tests and writing under a deadline ("writer's block"), using public restrooms, and dating. Generalized social phobias involve fear of a wide variety of social situations.

The symptoms of social phobia can be grouped into three categories. Bodily symptoms include sweating, blushing, trembling, and other physical signs of anxiety. Cognitive symptoms include maladaptive thoughts and beliefs about social situations. Behavioral symptoms include the freezing response and avoidance.

Social phobia affects literally millions of people. Mental health professionals' knowledge about this disorder is growing rapidly. Demonstrably effective methods now exist that can help you conquer your social fears.

2

The Causes of Social Phobia

Now that you've read about what a social phobia is, you should have a better idea about whether or not you have one. Perhaps you identified with one of the case examples we presented. Finding out that you are not alone can be reassuring; but several questions may still nag you. For instance, you may be asking yourself, "Why me?" or "How did I get a social phobia?" or "Why won't this problem just go away?"

Since it was only in 1980 that social phobia first appeared as an official diagnosis, there has been a limited amount of research into the problem. As of now, there is no single explanation accepted as the cause of social phobia. In fact, the only thing that most experts agree upon is that the origins of social phobia are unclear!

More than likely, you are less than enthusiastic about this news. But don't lose heart. Research is continuing, and there are already several promising ideas about what causes and maintains a social phobia. In this chapter, we will discuss some of these ideas. Both biology and environment have been proposed as contributors to the onset of social phobia.

How Do Social Phobias Develop?

Biological Contributions

Since the causes of social phobia became of interest to researchers, one important area of investigation has been the possible contributions of biology. In fact, some authorities believe that the primary cause of social phobia is biological. Biological explanations of social phobia have been drawn from biochemistry, genetics, and experimental psychology. Three major ideas about how biology might affect social phobias have been proposed: biochemical irregularities, genetic predispositions, and the evolution of biologically-based sensitivities to disapproval.

Biochemical Irregularities. Beginning with his work in 1966, David Sheehan, a psychiatrist and expert in the field of anxiety disorders, has argued that anxiety, including social anxiety, is a biologically-based "disease." The idea that anxiety was a disease held great promise and stimulated a great deal of research. Scientists and clinicians alike began to ask about how biochemical changes might influence the development of social phobia.

According to Dr. Sheehan, social phobia is simply a problem that involves panic attacks in social situations. You'll remember from the previous chapter that panic attacks are sudden surges of anxiety symptoms which typically include rapid heart rate, shortness of breath, dizziness, sweating, faintness, and to varying degrees, a feeling that you are going crazy, losing control, or dying. From a strictly biological perspective, panic is viewed as a dysregulation of those chemicals that allow our nervous system to work. This dysregulation sets off all sorts of false alarms. In support of this view, there is a large body of research which investigates how giving people certain chemicals in the laboratory can produce panic. Likewise, several medications are effective in treating panic, which also lends support to the role of biochemistry.

Dr. Sheehan asserts that people start avoiding social situations because they fear having another panic attack. Thus, a social phobia is a fear of experiencing one of these biological false alarms (in other words, panic) in social situations.

There are several problems with Dr. Sheehan's theory. First, for most people with a social phobia, the main concern is not the panic attack itself, but the potential disapproval of others who might judge their anxious behavior. Second, since the time when Dr. Sheehan put forward his disease model, laboratory research has found that chemicals (caffeine and sodium lactate, for example) that cause panic attacks in people prone to panic, do not produce panic attacks in individuals with social phobia. Third, many people with social phobia never develop panic attacks.

Despite the problems with Dr. Sheehan's theory, there is research that supports a biological explanation of the development of social phobia. For example, one study found differences between the physical symptoms reported by socially phobic and agoraphobic subjects (agoraphobics are people who avoid situations because they are afraid they will panic). Although the two groups overlapped on many symptoms, a team of British psychologists noted that the socially phobic subjects reported more blushing and muscle twitching—symptoms that tend to be visible to others—than did the agoraphobic subjects. In fact, this research suggests that people with a social phobia have a heightened physical reaction to those social situations that cause them anxiety. This was the case for Ron.

From the time he was a child, Ron had a problem with sweating. When he had to give a report in his third grade class, he remembered beads of sweat standing out on his forehead. Sweating became enough of a problem to cause his parents to take him to several doctors, but they could find no medical reason for Ron's sweating. As an adult, the problem only got worse. Any situation in which he had to be in contact or thought he would be in contact with people, particularly women, would cause Ron to sweat. His shirt would be soaked by the end of church. Once when he went to make a delivery for his boss, he was sweating so badly that a secretary asked him if it was raining outside.

Another way in which the symptoms of social phobia suggests a biological origin is that they typically do not go away over time, sometimes even when an effort has been made to overcome them. Ron, for example, remembers being anxious since the third grade. Like Ron, you may have found that over the years your symptoms have not diminished, in spite of your best efforts to conquer them. For some people, symptoms may even become worse over time. Researchers have been tempted to suggest that socially phobic individuals are far more sensitive to certain chemicals which the body releases in stressful situations. Likewise, these chemicals may be active in greater quantities or for a longer period of time for individuals with a social phobia. Unfortunately, studies attempting to test this theory have produced inconclusive results. We just do not know to what extent biochemical problems contribute to social phobia.

Genetic Predisposition. Another area of research that lends support to biological explanations of social phobia is family studies. In our clinic we frequently see people who report having family members who are anxious, who are "worriers," or who have social fears. Both clinical experience and research suggest that parents of individuals diagnosed with social phobia may themselves tend to be overprotective, socially fearful, and sensitive to the opinions of others. Consider your own family—might this be the case for you?

This has led some researchers to think that it is not just family environment, but genetics, which influences the development of social phobia. Unfortunately, there has been little research in this area. What research exists does suggest a genetic contribution to social phobia. In a study published in 1979, Dr. Svenn Torgerson found a greater incidence of social fears, such as concerns about being watched by strangers while working or eating, among identical twins rather than fraternal twins. This distinction is important, since identical twins have exactly the same genes, whereas fraternal twins do not. It is possible, then, that some aspects of social phobia may be inherited, but this does not seem to be true for all cases of social phobia. A great deal of research remains to be done in this area.

One case in which genetics seems to operate clearly is in those individuals who have Familial Essential Tremor—a common, dominantly inherited, fine motor tremor (shakiness in the hands). Dominantly inherited refers to the fact that if one of your parents has this condition, there's a strong likelihood that you will have it as well. The condition is worsened by caffeine and other stimulants, and may appear severe when you're under stress. If people who have this condition become self-conscious about the tremor, it's more likely to develop into a social phobia.

Inherent Sensitivity to Disapproval. Another idea about what causes social phobias comes from "preparedness theory." This theory suggests that human beings are biologically prepared to react to signs of disapproval from others. Your body is ready and waiting to react to what you perceive as a threatening situation. Fear, in this scenario, is an automatic reaction. According to preparedness theory, you are more reactive to, and more likely to develop a phobia about certain kinds of things.

One researcher, Dr. Arne Ohman, found that people are not only prepared to fear certain wild animals, but are also prepared to fear faces that can be interpreted as angry, critical, or rejecting. His research, corroborated by other studies, also discovered that these reactions are not voluntary, but more in the nature of automatic, occurring with great speed. People tend to associate these kinds of facial expressions with negative consequences. This type of automatic reaction is difficult to overcome.

One thing that has been found to contribute to this inherent sensitivity to disapproval is eye contact. Among animals, direct eye contact can be very frightening. When people are frightened, eye contact decreases. One of the problems many people with social phobia report is their discomfort making eye contact, especially with strangers.

It would seem then, that a human being's biological alarm system is finely tuned to respond to threats, perhaps including the threat of disapproval. Biochemistry, genes, and inborn sensitivities may combine to increase the chances that a social phobia will develop. However, when biology plays a role in your behavior, it doesn't mean that the outcome is preordained. As you will read later in this chapter, biological factors are likely to interact with other elements before a social phobia develops.

Environmental Contributions

As you read the above sections, you may have thought to yourself, "I've gone over and over the family tree and found no one with even the smallest complaint of anxiety. Am I the exception to these theories?" Probably not. Not all of the explanations for social phobia are biological. There are three ways in which your environment may also influence the development of a social phobia: through negative social experiences, by providing models of social fear behavior, and by transmitting incorrect information about social situations. Perhaps, as you read on, you will find an example that matches your own experience with social phobia.

Learning from Negative Social Experiences. Another explanation for so-cial phobia involves negative experiences in social situations. If you ex-perience a "blunder" or poor performance on your part as traumatic, you may become fearful when you find yourself in similar circumstances again. It is also likely that you will either dread or avoid other situations in which similar blunders or embarrassment could occur. Such dread can in itself compromise your performance in a future social situation.

Fears can develop from a series of merely disturbing events, the re-sult of a snowball effect of anxious situation on top of anxious situation. For others, a major traumatic experience ignites the social phobia: a single experience can "prime the pump" for future social anxiety. Consider what happened to Allison.

Ten-year-old Allison was eagerly looking forward to her school's Christmas choir performance. She knew that her mother, grandmother, and friends would be in the audience. When the big day finally came, Allison donned her choir robe and the bright red bow to wear around her neck. As the choir marched into the crowded auditorium, her excite-ment grew. Everything was going perfectly. However, as the choir began to sing, she began to feel flushed. Her cheeks grew warm and she began to have trouble breathing. She felt like she was going to faint. One of the teachers noticed that Allison was having trouble and helped her leave the stage. As she left, she saw several people in the audience laughing, and felt sure that the laughter was directed at her. The next week when the choir was to sing at a nursing home, Allison had a stomachache. Later, she began refusing to give book reports at the front of the classroom.

Allison viewed having to leave the stage as the worst thing that could have happened to her. She felt humiliated. She was especially em-barrassed because a teacher had to rescue her. She came to associate per-forming in front of others (and being nervous and leaving) with the risk of disapproval. Rather than take this risk, it was easier to avoid the situa-tion altogether.

Learning by Example. As we mentioned before, many socially phobic people report having parents who are anxious. It's possible that social fears can be learned by observing others with the same fear. One group of psychologists from the State University of New York at Albany found that parents of individuals with a social phobia were more socially fearful and concerned with the opinions of others than were the parents of people with another anxiety disorder. Although one interpretation of this information may support a genetic explanation of social phobia, another explanation deserves attention.

Children's earliest role models are their parents. Children imitate what their parents say and, probably more importantly, what they do. For example, if a parent looks anxious in social situations the child may begin to feel anxious in similar settings. In the same way, if a parent avoids social situations, the child may begin to fear and avoid them as well.

Although parents have significant impact, they're not a child's only role models. As individuals grow up, they're exposed to a wide range of people who display many different behaviors. You may have the opportunity to learn many useful and productive behaviors; unfortunately, we can't always select which ones to model. In general, people tend to be most influenced by others of importance in their lives (such as parents). This is particularly true when messages, both verbal and nonverbal, are repeated frequently.

It seems that social phobias can be learned, at least in part, by observing and modeling one's behavior on that of others. Not enough research has been done, though, to conclude whether this is indeed an important factor in the development of social phobia.

Learning from Incorrect Information. Another way in which the environment may contribute to a social phobia is by transmitting false information, which can lead you to exaggerate the danger involved in social situations. Every minute of your waking hours you are bombarded with information. Much but not all of this information is accurate. When misinformation is transmitted, it can lead to fear. Jeremy's story is a good example of how faulty information can go awry.

Jeremy was short. At his full adult height, he was 5'6" tall. Even as a child, he was always in the front row for his class picture—the row containing all of the short kids. He can remember his parents referring to him as their "perfect little man." Before he was even a teenager, Jeremy learned what it meant to be appropriately macho. Friends, relatives, and the media either subtly or not so subtly conveyed to him the stereotype of the American he-man. Jeremy grew to believe that he had to be tough and always project an image of masculinity. Unfortunately, Jeremy's body and voice, in his own opinion, failed to measure up. His parents' description of him seemed a contradiction in terms: how could a little man be perfect? He envied the football players at school. He was picked on by the bigger guys, and patronized by the girls. Coupled with his small size, he became concerned that people would think his voice effeminate, and he spent long hours alone in his room trying to affect a gravelly basso that did not come naturally to him.

Jeremy was particularly cautious when it came to dating. He was always on guard for the least indication that his date thought him unmanly. He affected a tough-guy persona that masked his real sensitivity; he often came across as defensive and argumentative. Dating became such a painful and embarrassing encounter for Jeremy that he finally just gave up.

Jeremy had based his beliefs about masculinity on two popular pieces of misinformation. The first was that all masculine men were tough and large, like the men in the Marlboro ads. This idea about what it means to be an adult male in American society doesn't take into account the wide variety of personal attributes and features that can be attractive to others. Jeremy believed that he could and should cast himself in the image of the Marlboro man. But since he was not by nature 6′5″ and brawny, he felt embarrassed and ashamed. He agonized that he wasn't measuring up to the stereotype: that he wasn't masculine enough.

Jeremy also acted on the incorrect assumption that he had to be perfect to be accepted by others. When he felt that his level of performance fell short of perfection, he was humiliated. It was important to Jeremy that he please the people around him, because otherwise he would risk their disapproval. Because both his goals were so unrealistic, Jeremy was very miserable indeed.

Holding on to a belief based on misinformation can lead to all sorts of problems. Just think how common phrases often misinform. For example: "You can't be too thin or too rich," or "If you can't do it right, don't do it at all," or "I could have died from embarrassment." Obviously, we have some investment in pointing out how the last statement can misinform you and misguide your behavior.

Perhaps one or more of these explanations of the possible causes of social phobia struck a chord with you. As we mentioned at the outset, several factors—both biological and environmental—may contribute to the development of a social phobia. In fact, the notion of a "combined factors" explanation of the origins of anxiety disorders is receiving more and more support from the scientific community. The more factors present in an individual case, the greater the chance of developing social fears. The notion of a single cause of social phobia seems more unlikely as new information on this disorder emerges.

Once They Start, Why Do Social Phobias Continue?

Knowing what originally caused a social phobia is only part of the picture. How severe the phobia becomes, and how long it lasts, depends upon a number of additional factors. In particular, how you interpret the social situations you fear and how you cope with those situations, determine whether your social phobia goes away, stays at a manageable level, or worsens with time. Now let's examine in more detail what things might determine the course of a social phobia.

Cognitive Factors: Misperceptions of Threat

How and what you think can have an enormous impact on your behavior. One person who makes a ridiculous slip of the tongue in front of friends may experience the mistake as an occasion for laughter, a moment of released tension, not worth a second thought. In contrast, the individual with a social phobia thinks of an identical experience as painfully humiliating, and may dwell on it for hours or even days afterwards. How can the same situation be interpreted so differently?

One explanation involves your thoughts and beliefs about social situations. Dr. Aaron Beck, who has written extensively in the area of cognitive therapy for depression and anxiety, considers the fear of disapproval to be at the core of social phobia. He observes that, unlike the case of many other phobias, there is a grain of truth in what the individual with a social phobia fears. In other words, it's true that anyone can make a mistake in a social situation. What further distinguishes a social phobia from some of the other phobias is that the thing that is dreaded (such as sweating, a poor performance, looking nervous) can readily be brought about by anxiety itself.

But there's more to the story. People with social phobias tend to perceive social situations differently than others do. Their fear of the situation is usually based on several misperceptions that typically take one of two forms: *distortions of probability* or *distortions of severity*. Probability distortions occur when you exaggerate the likelihood of something bad happening. In the case of social phobia, "something bad" is equated with disapproval. Severity distortions occur when you exaggerate how severe the consequences would be if something bad does indeed happen. Everyone falls prey to distortions of probability and severity from time to time. However, if these distortions get out of hand, you may become needlessly fearful and anxious. In Chapter 6, we'll closely examine these exaggerations of social danger, and show you how to work toward correcting them.

Maladaptive Coping

At some point in dealing with your problem with social phobia, you have probably said to yourself, "I just can't cope with this." It's much more likely, though, that you *can* cope: you're just not using the most constructive ways to deal with your anxiety, and your social fear persists despite efforts to keep it under control.

Maladaptive coping involves finding ways to "deal" with your social anxiety without solving the problem: you might avoid all potentially embarrassing social situations; you might medicate yourself with drugs or alcohol when facing a social situation is unavoidable. Both these strategies are maladaptive.

Although maladaptive coping often provides temporary relief, it can quickly become part of the problem. In the long run, such strategies feed your anxiety and keep your fear of disapproval alive. Let's examine some of the ways in which your way of coping might be making your phobia worse.

Avoiding Social Situations. One of the most common ways to deal with anxiety is to avoid it. Just think how easy your life would be if you didn't ever have to use a public restroom, eat in a restaurant, speak to a group, or go on a date! There would be no risk of disapproval to make you anxious. Of course, you would suffer in other ways. Your life would become more and more restricted. You might have problems on your job as well if you kept refusing to give a talk or take a client to lunch. Perhaps you're saying to yourself, "It's better not to take my client to lunch than to have her see me sweat into my salad." But what about that sale that fell through, that client you failed to win, that promotion you passed up? Was the temporary avoidance of discomfort really worth the price?

In addition to making your life more restricted, avoidance doesn't allow you to test your beliefs and discover whether you are exaggerating the probability or severity of experiencing disapproval. Every time you avoid a situation, or say to yourself, "I can't do this," you chip away at your self-confidence. The less confident you become, the more anxious you will be when you have to face a threatening activity. As your self-confidence decreases and your anxiety increases, you'll be more tempted to avoid the situation you fear. Finally, you may judge the anxiety as too much to deal with and actively avoid such situations altogether. Many of the clients we see have told us that their fear of public speaking doesn't make them anxious, because they don't ever give speeches! If you keep avoiding the situations you dread, your social fears are likely to remain entrenched.

Worry. Another factor that maintains a social phobia is worry. Now you may say to yourself, "Everybody worries." Of course, that's true: but there are reasonable and unreasonable kinds of worry. What we mean by worry here is dwelling obsessively on a future danger that may or may not occur. Such obsessive repetition of fearful thoughts is hard to turn off, and detracts from your ability to find solutions or effectively deal with your anxiety. Worry actually prolongs your anxiety and makes it more likely that you will feel anxious when you encounter the situation you fear.

So, what do you worry about when you have a social phobia? Basically, you worry about how you will perform, how others will react to you, and how you will handle their reaction. Jessie's story is a good example of how worry can affect social anxiety.

Jessie described herself as a worrier. She was always an excellent student, and in college was made Phi Beta Kappa. She was involved in several school organizations—her sorority, political groups, campus government, and so on. Despite active involvement in many social activities, Jessie was terrified to go out on a date. She would become anxious when conversations with an eligible man turned from the political to personal. She worried that she would say the wrong thing, or that someone would notice her nervousness. On a date she was even worse. She was convinced that she would become so anxious that she would become sick to her stomach, "totally lose it," and throw up—which she believed would cause her date to hate her. Of course, she reasoned, everyone on campus would then know that she had thrown up while out on a date. She would be completely humiliated, never be asked out again, and remain alone for the rest of her life.

Jessie is expecting the worst-case scenario, no matter what other possible outcomes exist. She has completely overlooked her strengths, focusing her attention instead on her fears. Her fears have escalated out of proportion to the situation. Instead of thinking the situation through dispassionately, Jessie worried about it, and the worry only made it worse. Her worry intensified her feelings of anxiety, and made going out on a date even harder.

It's easy to read about Jessie's situation and think, "She's blowing everything out of proportion." When Jessie wasn't nervous, she was also able to see how her worried thinking was catastrophic and irrational. But when she was feeling anxious, Jessie's worries seemed all too reasonable and real. At those times, it seemed entirely plausible that her worst fears would occur. Because of this lack of judgment at times of fear, worry can be a difficult process to interrupt unless you know how to identify that you are worrying and what you can do about it. The information and techniques in Chapters 5 and 6 can help you break the worry cycle.

Evaluating Your Performance While Trying To Perform. A common characteristic of social anxiety is to focus your concern on whether your behavior is being observed, on how well you are doing, and on what you believe others might be thinking of you. In other words, at the same time you are performing, you are busy evaluating your performance and your situation. Although this is a natural thing to do when you are anxious, it is also self-defeating.

Self-preoccupation acts to increase your level of anxiety. Perhaps even more importantly, the more you think about how well you're doing, or try to guess about other people's reactions, the less you can concentrate on what you're doing and the more likely it is that you'll make a mistake. Once having made a blunder, you may become even more anxious in the future. Self-preoccupation backfires by interfering with your performance and increasing the chance of making the mistake you most fear.

How Does It All Fit Together?

As you can see, many things contribute to the development and maintenance of a social phobia. The diagram below may help you keep track of the different factors discussed in this chapter.

Another example may also be of use in seeing how these factors fit together.

For as long as she could remember, Amanda disliked having to speak in front of groups. Nevertheless, she pushed herself, became a lawyer, and was active in public service. Her professional and volunteer activities caused her great discomfort, as both required public speaking. Gradually, the ordeal of public speaking became so uncomfortable for Amanda that she realized that she was going to have to switch careers or get professional help.

What might have caused Amanda's social phobia? Well, her mother was a worrier; so it's possible that Amanda inherited a tendency to be anxious, if not socially phobic. She also has a nightmarish memory of the first book report she ever gave in grade school. She'd been sick with a fever and the flu, but returned to school to make her presentation before she felt quite well again. She felt weak, shaky, and breathless standing before the class, and felt terrible about her performance afterwards. This negative experience could have contributed to her exaggerated fear of disapproval later on.

Once Amanda developed the phobia, what helped maintain it? First she exaggerated the probability that if she became breathless during a speech, she would meet with her audience's disapproval or derision. (The likelihood of this occurring was actually quite low.) She also exaggerated the severity of what would happen if someone did disapprove. She thought she might "fall apart," or even lose her job at her law firm. She also worried for days before her talk. During the ordeal itself, her attention kept wandering to her physical symptoms of anxiety, especially her dry throat. Amanda came to dread speaking engagements so much that on several occasions she became physically ill beforehand and had to call in sick.

For Amanda, the model of social phobia might look like this:

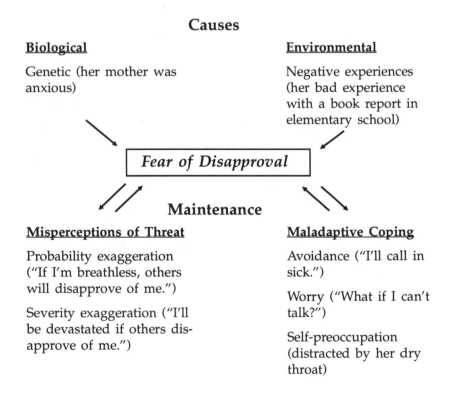

Causes

Biological

Genetic (her mother was anxious)

Environmental

Negative experiences (her bad experience with a book report in elementary school)

Fear of Disapproval

Maintenance

Misperceptions of Threat

Probability exaggeration ("If I'm breathless, others will disapprove of me.")

Severity exaggeration ("I'll be devastated if others disapprove of me.")

Maladaptive Coping

Avoidance ("I'll call in sick.")

Worry ("What if I can't talk?")

Self-preoccupation (distracted by her dry throat)

Summary

The fund of knowledge about the causes of social phobia is still growing. There is no one theory that everyone agrees on, and no single theory that research clearly supports. Our model of social phobia attempts to integrate various perspectives. Some people may have a biological vulnerability to social phobias, which is expressed only when several other environmental elements come into play. Once these causal factors are present, there are several ways in which you may unintentionally make the phobia worse. The way in which you think about a feared situation, especially if you exaggerate its probability or severity, will worsen your social fears. Certain coping strategies—such as worrying about or avoiding the situation—may be maladaptive, actually making things worse in the long run.

SECTION II

Preparing for Recovery

In Section I, you learned about the nature and causes of social phobia. The chapters in this section are designed to help you prepare for recovery. First, in Chapter 3, you will learn how to set goals and objectives. Next, Chapter 4 will teach you how to assess your fears and develop a recovery plan. Both of these chapters are very important because they lay the groundwork for the rest of the steps required to overcome your social phobia.

3

Setting Your Goals and Objectives

Before you set out to overcome a social phobia, you first need to develop your goals and objectives. Without them, your efforts will lack focus and direction. Goals and objectives are, in essence, your map to help you navigate the road to recovery. Goals tell you where you're generally headed, while objectives let you know exactly when you've arrived.

Defining Your Goal

The first step you need to complete is to define a goal. Having a goal answers the question, "What do I want to accomplish?" You might be surprised at how often people jump into action without first having carefully considered this question. You might feel that the answer is obvious. "I want to get rid of my social phobia." Of course, this is a desirable goal, but it is far too general to be a useful goal. A useful goal must be specific.

To help you determine your specific goal, ask yourself these questions:

- What type of social situation do I want to stop avoiding?

- How do I want to feel in that social situation?

As you can see from these questions, a specific goal will contain two components: 1) The situation you want to learn to handle better, and 2) How you want to feel in that situation.

Here are some common examples of specific goals:

- I want to give public presentations comfortably.

- I want to go on dates with minimal anxiety.

- I want to eat in restaurants with relative ease.

- I want to use public restrooms without fear of embarrassment.

Now that you have some examples, think about what goal you want to work on and jot it down in the space below. Again, make sure it contains both the type of situation you want to master and how you want to feel in the situation.

*My goal:*_____

One important note about your goal before we move on: It's important that your goal be realistic and achievable. Tackling a social phobia with unrealistic expectations will only lead to frustration and disappointment. For example, it is not realistic to expect to eliminate all anxiety in all situations. You may be able to become more comfortable in social situations, but everyone experiences some anxiety. It is equally unhelpful to set too high a standard for your performance. A realistic goal does not demand that you behave perfectly. Human beings are not perfect. Striving to give a flawless speech or to always say the right thing is a setup for failure because you have set a goal that is impossible to achieve. Sure it's nice to do your best, but it's even more important to become comfortable with the fact that we're all imperfect by nature. Okay, look back at your goal again. Make sure you've worded it in such a way that it's realistic.

What If I Have More Than One Goal?

Granted, many of you may have more than one goal. Perhaps you want to learn to be more comfortable in dating situations, but you also want to learn to give public presentations with ease. Although it would be nice if you could achieve all of your goals simultaneously, it usually doesn't work this way. Typically, it makes more sense to work on certain goals first, and others later on. Working on more than one goal at once can dilute your efforts, making it difficult to see progress. In contrast, when you work on one goal at a time, you can focus all your energy on one area. You may even be surprised that by achieving one goal, your other goals will be much easier to accomplish later on.

So if you have more than one goal, how do you decide where to begin? Putting your goals in order of importance is one approach, but this is not the only issue to consider. Also consider which of your goals might be more realistic to tackle first. Some people may prefer to tackle an easy goal first, thus getting off to a good, smooth start, and getting their feet wet slowly. Others may want to work on a more challenging goal first, to get it out of the way early on. Still others may have less latitude in making a choice. If your job requires you to give a speech in a month, it's obviously going to be more important for you to work on that goal first, even though you may also want to learn to ask someone out for a date.

Ultimately, the priority you give each of your goals is up to you. Keep in mind that there's really no right or wrong order. If you start working on one goal and later realize that you need to work on a different goal first, you can easily make the switch. The purpose of establishing priorities for your goals is to have a game plan, but game plans can always change. We suggest that you work through the methods in this book using one goal (switching to another goal only if necessary). Later, you can work on achieving your other goals as well.

Defining Your Objectives

After you've set the goal you want to work toward, the next step is to define your objectives. Sometimes in everyday speech the words "goal" and "objective" are used interchangeably, but we're giving them two distinct meanings in this context. Defining your goal answers the question, "What do I want to accomplish?" Defining your objective answers the question, "How will I know when I have accomplished my goal?" or "What will be different once I reach my goal?" Objectives are important because they are the signals that will tell you when you have been successful. Objectives also help personalize your goal and give more direction to your recovery plan.

Typically, objectives involve changes in specific behaviors, thoughts, and feelings that will occur when you accomplish your goal. You may have several different objectives for a single goal. For example, if your goal is to be able to eat in public, your objectives might include accepting invitations to go out to eat, sitting through an entire dinner in the middle of a crowded restaurant, and becoming comfortable eating lunch at the company cafeteria with business colleagues. As you can see, when you have reached your objectives, you will have achieved your goal.

Let's look at another example of developing objectives for a specific goal.

Goal:

I want to be more outgoing and comfortable at social gatherings.

Objectives:

- I will feel less anxious when I am introduced to a stranger.

- I will be able to make eye contact.

- I won't turn down invitations to family gatherings.

- I will feel like I can hold my own in a conversation.

- I will stop assuming that I am saying the wrong thing all the time.

- I will make new friends.

Can you see how objectives help define and personalize a goal? Can you also see how objectives guide you, letting you know what kinds of things you need to do to begin your recovery?

Before you set out to write your own objectives, take a look at the goal and objectives set out by Ginny, a 28-year-old mother of two elementary-school-age children.

Goal:

I want to be more outgoing and confident in my work as a parent and in my role in the community.

Objectives:

- I will be less afraid to sit up front at church.

- I will return to my volunteer activities.

- I will talk to the other parents when carpooling.

- I will be able to introduce myself at meetings.

Now that you've seen how Ginny defined her goal and objectives, try a hand at writing your own.

My Goal and Objectives

Goal:

_____

Objectives:

- _____

- _____

- _____

- _____

- _____

A Practice Example

Although setting your goal and writing out objectives might seem like an easy task at first glance, it can be more difficult than you'd think.

If you're having trouble, don't give up. Here's an example that will let you go through the whole process once more.

Tom, a 40-year-old police officer with a strong fear of public speaking, had become adept at creating reasons to avoid participating in public education programs sponsored by the police department. These would have required him to address community gatherings—something certain to make him nervous, even panicky. Most of the other officers in his small police department regularly volunteered for the informational talks on such topics as crime prevention; indeed, this was expected of officers. Tom, however, made clever excuses whenever his lack of involvement was noted.

These were not the only situations Tom avoided. He was always quiet at departmental meetings, never giving his opinion or asking a question. He dropped out of a college class recommended by his superiors when he found out that three class presentations were required, even though this hurt his chances for promotion. Similarly, Tom was unwilling to serve as a reader at church on Sundays due to his fear. He would not even consider activities that made it necessary for him to address a group, even briefly or informally. He preferred that people see him as uncommitted, disorganized, or even rude, rather than view him as anxious, awkward, or foolish. And, of course, he didn't want to experience the sweating, rapid heart rate, shakiness, and other symptoms he associated with public scrutiny. Tom engaged in this pattern of avoidance for years.

Eventually, an incident occurred that left Tom determined to overcome his phobia. He was asked to say grace before dinner at a small gathering of his relatives. But he was so terrified that he refused. Afterward, Tom felt a new sense of anger and shame at the extent to which his fears controlled him. He couldn't even say a simple prayer in front of a few family members! Finally, he decided to stop running away from his problem.

Tom's problem is a common example of social phobia. We will be referring back to his problem throughout the rest of this book as we teach you the various principles and techniques involved in the recovery process. Even if your phobia is not exactly like Tom's, you'll be able to understand the process and then apply it to your particular situation.

Initially, Tom wrote out his goal like this:

My Goal: I want to be a great public speaker and never feel nervous.

What do you think about the goal Tom set for himself? Can you see how the wording could be improved? Tom, somewhat reluctantly, reconsidered his goal to see if it might be unrealistic or unachievable. This was a tough task for him. It's hard to let go of a goal you really want to achieve, even if deep down you know that it's not realistic. After a lot of thought, Tom conceded that his goal was written in a way that doomed him to failure. How could he expect to "never" be afraid or nervous, when even polished performers feel pangs of anxiety before going on stage? Wasn't he putting a lot of pressure on himself by setting a goal to be a "great" public speaker?

Here is Tom's revised goal and the objectives he set for himself.

Goal:

I want to become more comfortable with public speaking.

Objectives:

- I will accept invitations to give public education programs.

- I will assist in services at church.

- I will ask questions and express my opinion in department meetings.

- I will say grace at family get-togethers.

Notice how Tom's goal is much more manageable now. No longer does he have to become a "great" public speaker in order to succeed; and he can forgive himself a normal amount of nervousness. His objectives are also realistic and attainable, and will allow him to recognize when he has achieved his goal. Hopefully, going through the process with Tom helped clarify any confusion about defining your goal and setting your objectives.

Summary

The purpose of this chapter is to start you on your way to a recovery plan by helping you define your goal and set your objectives. Your goal is best expressed by a general statement about what you want to accomplish in overcoming a social phobia. Goals should be specific and contain two components: 1) The social situation you want to master, and 2) How you want to feel in that situation. Your goal should be accompanied by several objectives. Objectives in this context are those changes in your behavior, thoughts, or feelings that you expect to occur when your goal is achieved. Objectives help you gauge your progress toward achieving your goal. With your goal and objectives clearly stated, you're now ready to move on to the next step in preparing for recovery—assessing your fears.

4

Assessing Your Fears and Developing Your Recovery Plan

The next step in preparing for recovery is to develop a clear understanding of your specific social phobia or set of fears. Each person's problem is unique. Any two people will have different strengths from which to draw, and different obstacles to face, as they attempt to recover from their phobias. A successful recovery plan takes these obstacles and strengths into account. In the previous chapter, you set your goals and objectives. In this chapter, we'll show you how to develop a comprehensive plan of action that will allow you to achieve your goals. In short, we'll help you determine which parts of this book you'll want to emphasize in your efforts to overcome your social phobia.

Questions To Help You Assess Your Fears

The first step in developing your personalized recovery plan is to thoroughly assess yourself and your fears. Only by taking a thorough look at your particular symptoms can you hope to overcome your fears. Otherwise, your recovery efforts may result in frustration and disappointment. If you carefully proceed through the questions and assessment forms in this chapter, you'll greatly increase your chances for success.

1. *How Does My Body React To Disapproval?* As you learned in Chapter 1, most people experience physical symptoms when they are afraid or anxious. What symptoms do you experience? The following checklist is designed to help you answer this question. If you are unsure of your symptoms, try entering one of the situations you fear and notice what

bodily reactions you have. Read the list of symptoms below and check those that you experience when you are socially anxious.

Bodily Symptoms of Social Phobia

☐ Rapid heart rate   ☐ Dry mouth

☐ Shortness of breath   ☐ Urinary urgency

☐ Abdominal distress   ☐ Tingling sensations

☐ Sweating   ☐ Muscle twitching

☐ Blushing   ☐ Chest pain

☐ Trembling or shaking   ☐ Numbness

☐ Dizziness or feeling faint   ☐ Hot flashes or chills

☐ Tense muscles   ☐ Other:_____

☐ Choking or lump in throat   ☐ Other:_____

Most people with social phobias experience at least some of these physical symptoms when they are anticipating, or actually entering, a feared social situation. If you checked a number (or all) of these physical symptoms, don't despair. You can learn to handle your body's reactions to fear effectively. Chapter 5 will teach you an anxiety management skill that can help you feel more physically comfortable when facing your fears. In addition, some people may want to include medication in their recovery plan to help manage their symptoms. Before deciding to do this, however, please read Chapter 16.

One important word of caution: Sometimes physical symptoms mask a medical problem. If you have not had a recent physical examination, please make an appointment with your doctor to make sure that this is not the case for you.

2. *How Does My Mind React To Disapproval?* You learned in Chapter 1 that your mind, as well as your body, can react strongly when fear is present. Most noticeably, you begin to experience fearful thoughts or *cognitions*. Below is a list of some of the cognitive symptoms of social phobia you may experience. Place a checkmark next to any of these thoughts you experience when you're socially anxious.

Cognitive Symptoms of Social Phobia

☐ I look out of place.

☐ I sound stupid.

☐ I don't fit in.

☐ I'm blowing it.

☐ I know they hate me.

☐ I look ugly.

☐ I look fat.

☐ I'll be rejected.

☐ I appear incompetent.

☐ Others are talking about me.

☐ I'm unlovable.

☐ I look nervous.

☐ I'm so embarrassed.

☐ I'm too quiet.

☐ I sound boring.

☐ I'm such a klutz.

☐ I'm unattractive.

☐ No one likes me.

☐ Other:_____

☐ Other:_____

You may experience other fearful thoughts besides these. Feel free to add to the list any other thoughts that pop into your head when you become anxious in social situations. Now look back over your list. Are these thoughts disturbing to you? Do they keep coming back and bothering you? At the time you experience them, do you believe they might be true? If you answered yes to any of these questions, you'll want to learn more about handling your mind's reaction to the fear of disapproval. Following the guidelines in Chapter 6 should be a major focus of your recovery plan.

3. *How Do I Try To Avoid Disapproval?* You've already assessed how your body and mind react to disapproval. Now you'll examine how you behave when you're scared. Typically, people attempt to avoid the things they fear. It's natural for you to avoid situations that make you uncomfortable. However, as you've already learned, avoidance only prolongs the life of a social phobia.

It's easy to see how avoiding a situation altogether can keep you from becoming less afraid of it. There are less obvious forms of avoidance, though. Consider the various ways in which you engage in what's called *partial avoidance*. Partial avoidance refers to limiting what you will or will not do in certain social situations. Let's take Wayman's case by way of illustration.

Wayman attended lots of parties and dinners with his wife, despite a strong social phobia. Although he never refused to attend these activities, Wayman avoided introducing himself to strangers, would only agree to stay for a maximum of two hours, and insisted that his wife never leave his side for more than a few moments. As you can see, this kind of partial avoidance can be quite disabling. Other examples of partial avoidance are having to restrict yourself to a certain safe location, refusing work promotions that would require additional social demands, drinking alcohol, refraining from eye contact with others, and mentally distracting yourself from anxiety or the social situation creating it. Carefully consider the checklist below and mark all the behavioral symptoms of partial avoidance that apply to your social phobia.

Behavioral Symptoms of Social Phobia
I engage in partial avoidance of my feared social situation by…

☐ Turning up the radio

☐ Thinking about other things

☐ Limiting my opportunities

☐ Using other distractions

☐ Staying only a certain length of time

☐ Using alcohol or drugs

☐ Daydreaming

☐ Staying close to a safe person

☐ Only going to safe places

☐ Not making eye contact

☐ Setting other special conditions

☐ Other:_____

Taking time to thoughtfully complete this checklist will be helpful when you reach Section IV of this book. Chapters 7, 8, 9, and 10 are all devoted to helping you reverse self-defeating patterns of avoidance, including partial avoidance. They are crucial to include in your recovery plan.

4. *Why Should I Change My Reactions To Disapproval?* This is an important question to answer, because without the incentive to change, you will be unwilling to devote the time and energy necessary to do so. Below, or on your own sheet of paper, write out all of the reasons to overcome your social phobia (for example, to get a new job, to have more friends, to stop feeling lonely, to go back to school, and so on).

Reasons To Overcome My Social Phobia

1._____

2._____

3._____

4._____

5._____

6._____

7._____

8._____

9._____

10._____

Now examine your list. The more reasons you have, and the more important, immediate, and pressing they seem, the more likely you are to successfully complete your recovery plan.

Remember—recovery is not easy. So as you read your list of reasons to recover, you must feel that they clearly outweigh the discomfort and inconvenience of whatever steps you must take to lessen your fear of disapproval. If you have some doubts about whether your incentive for recovery is sufficient, you'll want to read Chapter 14. In this chapter, we offer suggestions for increasing your incentive to recover.

5. *What Else Should I Consider?* There are several other things to consider when developing a recovery plan. As you attempt to establish your commitment to recovery, learn to handle the mental and physical aspects of anxiety more effectively, and reverse your tendency to avoid social situations, other obstacles may get in your way. In some cases, social phobias are partially due to a lack of certain skills that are necessary to perform adequately in social situations. If you feel that deficits in skills such as initiating a conversation, being able to express your opinion assertively, or preparing an effective public presentation might be contributing to your social phobia, pay special attention to Chapter 11.

Some people find that stress from other areas of their life makes it difficult for them to deal with their social anxiety. In these instances, it can be beneficial to learn more about how to manage stress more effectively. If you feel that this might be the case for you, please read Chapter 12. There are also other problems—such as depression, alcohol abuse, and other kinds of anxiety—that can impede your progress. Chapter 13 addresses many of these issues.

Finally, even though you may be successful initially in recovering from your social phobia, sometimes the symptoms can return, to a greater or lesser extent, at a later point in your life. This is a very common occurrence and should not be cause for concern. However, there are things you can do to help ensure that the progress you make is maintained. Strategies for maintaining your progress and dealing with setbacks are outlined in Chapter 15. It is also important for you to know that there are other resources available when problems arise. Chapter 16 provides information on the role of medication in the treatment of social phobia, and Chapter 17 can help you find a therapist for additional support and assistance in your recovery.

Developing Your Recovery Plan

By now you have some idea of which chapters in this book you'll need to utilize in achieving the goals and objectives of your recovery. Although there's nothing wrong with reading this book in its entirety, you'll want to focus your energy on the chapters that are most relevant to your needs.

Take some time to review the goal and objectives you set in Chapter 3; and write down which chapters from this book you will be focusing on for your recovery plan. We'll illustrate how this should look with the example of Bernard, a 20-year-old single male whose social phobia involves dating. Bernard's recovery plan is outlined below:

Goal:

I want to feel more comfortable participating in social activities involving single women my age.

Objectives:

- I will join a singles group at my synagogue.
- I will initiate conversations with women.
- I will ask a woman out for a date.

Plan:

- I will read and follow the procedures outlined in Chapters 5, 6, 7, 8, 9, 10, and 11.

Of course, this looks easy! However, actually following these procedures amounted to a very comprehensive plan. Bernard selected each chapter for a specific reason. He felt that in order to overcome his social phobia, it was important that he learn to handle more effectively the reactions of his body and mind to fear (Chapters 5 and 6), to change his pattern of avoiding contact with women (Chapters 7-10), and to sharpen his conversational and dating skills (Chapter 11). Once Bernard achieves his goals, we would also recommend that he read Chapter 15, on how to maintain your gains.

Let's go through one more example before you write your own recovery plan. Remember Tom, the police officer from the previous chapter? Here's what his complete recovery plan looks like.

Tom's Recovery Plan

Goal:

I want to become more comfortable with public speaking.

Objectives:

- I will accept invitations to give public education programs.

- I will assist in services at church.

- I will ask questions and express my opinion in department meetings.

- I will say grace at family get-togethers.

Plan:

- I will read and follow the procedures outlined in Chapters 5, 6, 7, 8, 9, 10, 11, 13, and 15.

Tom selected Section III (Chapters 5 and 6), Learning Skills To Handle the Fear of Disapproval, because he knew that he needed to learn to manage his physical and cognitive reactions to fearful social situations before he could have the confidence to speak in public. Then he selected all the chapters in Section IV, Facing Your Fear of Disapproval (Chapters 7-10). We feel that the majority of people reading this book will need to focus much of their energy on Sections III and IV, just like Bernard and Tom. These chapters will form the core of most people's recovery plans.

Of course, you should tailor your plan to meet your own individual needs. Tom decided to include Chapter 11, primarily for the suggestions offered there on giving presentations. He knew that this would greatly help him in his job. He also included Chapter 13, because he was experiencing some problems with depression. Finally, Tom recognized that Chapter 15 would be important to ensure that he didn't let any setbacks impede his progress.

Now it's time for you to write a recovery plan of your own. If your plan is as well thought out as Tom's, you're likely to be successful. Once you've completed this task, you're ready to begin your recovery. Good luck!

My Recovery Plan

Goal:

_____

Objectives:

- _____

- _____

- _____

- _____

- _____

Plan:

- _____

Summary

In this chapter we've attempted to help you assess your fears, behaviors, and goals and, based on these, to develop an effective recovery plan. A set of questions helped you determine which chapters in this book will be most relevant to your individual needs. These are the chapters to which you'll want to devote the most time and energy. We then showed you how to write a recovery plan. If you have followed these procedures carefully, you are now ready to begin the process of recovery, and you can move on to Chapter 5.

SECTION III

Learning Skills To Handle the Fear of Disapproval

In the preceding section, you took stock of what you need to learn in order to master your social fears. In this section, we will teach you how to deal with fear itself. Chapter 5 will show you how to manage the physical symptoms of anxiety. Chapter 6 will help you explore and change thoughts that contribute to the fear of disapproval.

5

Handling Your Body's Reaction to Fear

At this point, you've set your sights on feeling more comfortable in social situations. You've taken inventory of your social fears and set realistic goals. This chapter, along with the next, lays the groundwork for achieving those goals. Before you face your fears, however, you need to know that you can cope with your physical reactions to fear. Otherwise, it may seem like trying to jump into deep water without first learning how to swim.

Acute Versus Chronic Bodily Reactions to Fear

When we talk about your body's reaction to fear, we mean the physical sensations you feel just prior to, or upon entering, a dreaded social situation. For example, imagine that you're just about to give a speech. Your heart may be racing and you may be sweating. These symptoms are related to *acute* anxiety, because they tend to come on suddenly and feel quite intense. In contrast, *chronic* bodily symptoms of anxiety may be less intense but more frequent and extended over a longer period of time. These include such complaints as headaches, stomachaches, fatigue, and irritability.

The distinction between acute and chronic bodily symptoms of anxiety is not always quite this neat and tidy. For example, someone with high levels of chronic anxiety may be more prone to experiencing bouts of acute anxiety. For our purposes here, however, we'll discuss acute and chronic anxiety as separate phenomena.

This chapter focuses on a basic acute anxiety management technique called *paced breathing*. Everyone reading this book will likely benefit from learning this important skill. In Chapter 12, we'll teach you techniques to cope with chronic anxiety, which is perhaps better known as stress. Although most people would benefit from Chapter 12, it's not mandatory reading for everyone attempting to overcome social phobia.

Some Hints Before You Get Started

We'd like to offer you a few tips to think about before you get started. First, consider the title of this chapter—Handling Your Body's Reaction To Fear. Notice that we didn't call it Learning How To Get Rid of Anxiety. As we've stated before, getting rid of anxiety is neither an achievable nor a realistic goal. After all, there are many situations in which feeling anxious is absolutely appropriate. Although getting rid of all anxiety is not possible, handling anxiety is both achievable and desirable. Accepting that anxiety cannot be eliminated, and that you can still function effectively despite being afraid, is an important lesson to learn. In time, you'll notice that, while you're still apt to feel some anxiety in certain social situations, the intensity of your bodily symptoms will decrease considerably. Most importantly, with practice, your self-confidence will increase, and you'll be better prepared to enter the social situations you fear.

Our second tip involves anxiety management and sleep. For many people, right before bedtime seems like a good time for practicing coping skills. It's a quiet time, when the kids are asleep, you've finished your chores, and the phone is unlikely to ring. You may even be thinking about using these skills to help you get to sleep. Unfortunately, pairing anxiety management skills and sleep is not a good idea. The point of these skills is to help reduce anxiety—not to associate anxiety reduction with sleep. If you want to practice before bedtime, leave some time between when you practice and when you go to sleep. Get up and wash your face or let the dog out, for example, after you practice. Don't just roll over, turn off the lights, and go to sleep after practicing your skills.

Finally, remember that the paced breathing technique we will teach you is only one technique out of many that are available. Although we have found that this is the simplest and most effective acute anxiety management technique for a majority of people, it's not the only method. Give paced breathing a try; but if it doesn't work for you, some of the stress management techniques in Chapter 12 can be adapted to help you cope with acute anxiety.

The Paced Breathing Technique

We consider paced breathing to be an essential skill. Once you have mastered paced breathing, you will have a reliable tool that will enable you to confront some of the situations you fear.

So what is paced breathing? Paced breathing refers to a slower, more regular rate of breathing. When doing paced breathing, you breathe from your diaphragm rather than from your upper chest. (Your diaphragm is the very large and strong muscle that separates your chest cavity from your abdominal cavity. It's also the muscle that's responsible for your being able to inhale and exhale.)

Perhaps you're saying to yourself, "I know how to breathe. I've been doing it all of my life!" You're only half right. Yes, you know how to breathe but, if you're like many people who have problems with anxiety, you aren't breathing properly. As a quick test, take one hand and place it just above your belt or your waist. Place your other hand in the middle of your chest, right below your collarbone. Now, breathe as you normally would. Which hand is moving the most? If the hand that's on your chest is doing most of the moving, read the following section carefully—because you are among the many people who can benefit from paced breathing.

How Paced Breathing Works

There is probably not a single adult alive who hasn't heard the words, "Stand up straight. Hold your stomach in." In an effort to have good posture and to look your best, you may have acquired a bad habit. Instead of breathing from your diaphragm—and moving your stomach in and out—you've ended up breathing from your upper chest. Think for a minute about what a baby looks like when he or she is asleep. When babies breathe, they move their bellies. That kind of "belly breathing" is coming from the diaphragm rather than the upper part of the chest. Likewise, when you sleep, you breathe abdominally.

Why is this important? When you breathe primarily from your upper chest, you increase the risk of hyperventilating. Most people think of hyperventilation as panting. Panting, or gasping for air, is one form of hyperventilation, but it's not the only way you can hyperventilate. Other forms include sighing, yawning, holding your breath, or any forceful deep breath (either forceful on the inhale or exhale).

Shallow, chest-level breathing creates a problem. Unknowingly, you may be chronically hyperventilated. Hyperventilation alters your body's chemistry ever so slightly. It changes the balances of such chemicals as carbon dioxide, calcium, oxygen, and bicarbonate. Although these alterations are by no means life threatening, they do have important consequences for those of you who are sensitive to physical symptoms of anxiety. The results of hyperventilation take the form of many of the symptoms commonly associated with anxiety. For example, shortness of breath, lightheadedness, faintness, clamminess, tingling or numbness in your extremities, and derealization (feeling like you're walking around in a dream) are just some of the symptoms that result from hyperventilation.

If you're slightly hyperventilated to begin with, when you become anxious, there's a natural tendency to breathe even more quickly. As a result, you become more hyperventilated, thus creating a vicious cycle. You then experience all of those unpleasant symptoms of anxiety. You may find that breathing retraining alone may help to relieve many of your physical symptoms.

Learning Paced Breathing

Learning how to breathe more effectively is really not all that difficult. There are three key elements to keep in mind.

1. *Breathe slowly.* Ideally, you should be able to slow your rate of respiration down to eight-to-ten breaths per minute. It's not necessary to count, though. Simply concentrate on deliberately slowing down the pace of your breathing. And don't worry—you can't breathe too slowly! Concentrating on your breathing in this manner has the added benefit of shifting your attention away from any symptoms of anxiety that you may be experiencing.

2. *Breathe through your nose.* Breathing through your nose helps to prevent you from inadvertently hyperventilating. It's much easier to revert to shallow, upper chest breathing if you are breathing through your mouth. Also, it's impossible to gulp air if you breathe through your nose. Despite what you may have read elsewhere, do not inhale or exhale through your mouth. Instead, keep your mouth closed and breathe through your nose.

3. *Alternate paced and normal breathing.* There is a normal balance between chest and diaphragmatic breaths. Don't expect that every single breath should come from your abdomen. The average number of diaphragmatic to upper chest breaths is four-to-one. Set your goals to shift the ratio in the favor of abdominal breathing.

There are two exceptions to these rules. First, if you have a chronic respiratory condition, such as emphysema or asthma, learning these techniques may be more difficult or complicated. If you have any medical problem that involves your breathing or your lungs, consult your physician first before learning paced breathing or any new breathing technique. In many cases, physicians agree that learning these methods can be beneficial to individuals with respiratory problems; but this may not be so in your case. Check with your doctor first.

Second, there are times when you shouldn't worry about breathing through your chest versus your diaphragm. During and for a period of time after strenuous exercise, you'll find that you're breathing hard and using both upper chest and abdominal breathing. This is normal. Your body needs oxygen in large quantities, since oxygen is one of the fuels you use when you're expending energy. Don't try to force yourself at such times to breathe only from your diaphragm. Just let your body do what it needs to. When you've completely cooled down from your exercise, you can monitor your breathing.

Getting Started

There are a few preliminary steps involved in learning the basics of slow-paced diaphragmatic breathing.

Step One. The first step is to find a quiet spot where you'll be free from interruptions. You'll need about 15 minutes twice each day during which you won't be distracted or interrupted—no telephones, doorbells, or pets to pounce in your lap. So, shut the door, unplug the phone, and give Fido a bone.

Step Two. Next, get comfortable. Pick a spot where you can sit or lie comfortably. You want to make sure that your back feels supported and you don't feel too constricted by the arms of a chair or tight clothing, for example. A bed, the floor, or a reclining chair are all good places.

Step Three. In order to assess your progress, you'll have to learn to rate your level of anxiety. This is your own personal interpretation of anxiety that you rate on a 0-10 scale. A 10 on the scale is the most anxious or afraid you've ever been in your entire life. A 0, on the other hand, is the most relaxed you've ever been. Don't worry if at first it doesn't feel like you're doing the ratings right. It takes a few times to get the hang of it. Remember, too, that it's your personal rating system—your anxiety level of 5 is different than a 5 for anyone else. Take a look at the Scale for Rating Intensity of Anxiety below. This scale should help you to be more precise in rating your anxiety level.

Scale for Rating Intensity of Anxiety

0	1	2	3	4	5	6	7	8	9	10

NONE	MILD	MODERATE	SEVERE	VERY SEVERE
Relaxed, no discomfort	Not quite relaxed, just noticeable discomfort	Definite discomfort but managing it	Extremely uncomfortable: feel it is becoming unmanageable	Worst I have ever felt— overwhelming

Using the scale, take a second or two and rate your anxiety level right now. Throughout the process of becoming an expert in anxiety management, you'll be rating your anxiety level and keeping track of your progress on the Anxiety Management Log below. You'll rate your anxiety level both before and after each practice session. There are also sections on the log to indicate the date and time of your practice session, how long you spent, and where you practiced. There's also a section for comments, where you can note if you experienced any problems, interruptions, or a particularly successful practice session. These ratings are important, since they will help you gauge your mastery of these skills.

Step Four. Now that you've gotten a taste of how to rate your level of anxiety, a final comment is in order. Many people want to know whether or not to close their eyes when doing anxiety management exercises. The answer is that it's up to you. We've found that closing your eyes may help you concentrate on the exercise and not be distracted by what's happening around you. Ultimately, though, during practice sessions, it's your choice. Keep in mind that you'll also be using paced breathing at times when you are in social situations with your eyes open. It may be easier to apply the technique then if you've done some of your practice with your eyes open.

Practicing Paced Breathing

Practicing paced breathing is actually quite easy. Begin by lying on your back. Place your hand or something light (like a box of tissues or a paperback book) on your stomach between your belly button and the bottom of your rib cage. Concentrate on making your stomach move your hand or the object. If you are successful, you should be able to get your stomach to move toward the ceiling. It's that simple! Once you've become proficient at paced breathing, you won't need to keep watching your stomach to know that you're breathing diaphragmatically.

Some people have a little difficulty coordinating their breathing with moving their stomach. Should this be the case for you, don't become frustrated. Your body knows how to breath diaphragmatically—you do it every night when you go to sleep. Just remember the two basic rules: make sure you're breathing slowly, and breathing through your nose. Concentrating on these two rules should help you master this skill.

As we mentioned in Step One above, you need to set aside two 15-minute periods each day in order to master the skill. If you are able to practice according to the schedule we've suggested, it should take you approximately one-to-two weeks to master the basics of this skill. While it's not a catastrophe if you practice less, it will take you longer to effectively use paced breathing.

We've also found that "mini-practices" are of great benefit, since they act as a reminder throughout the day to breathe properly. Think of an activity you frequently engage in during the day and which can serve as a cue to help you remember to breathe. If you drive a lot, waiting at

Make photocopies of the log before you begin filling it in.

Anxiety Management Log

Date & Time	Beginning Anxiety Level (0-10)	Amount of Time Practiced	Ending Anxiety Level (0-10)	Where Practiced	Comments or Problems

traffic lights presents a good opportunity. Other possible cues might be when you hang up the telephone, when you open or close the refrigerator door, when commercials come on during a TV show, or when you enter or leave a room. Some people place a small, self-adhesive dot on their wristwatch to help them remember to breath every time they check the time. You may have other cues that you can add to this list. Simply pick one or two and, as you go through the day, cue yourself to breathe slowly and deeply for 15-30 seconds!

Using Paced Breathing When You're Anxious

There are no doubt times when your anxiety level shoots up from its usual state to near-panic or panic proportions. These are the times when you need an immediate way to reduce your level of discomfort. Paced breathing can help at those times.

Remember Tom, the police officer with a strong fear of public speaking? So far, we've followed his progress through setting his goals and taking stock of his fears. Let's see how he used his paced breathing skills.

Tom was fairly faithful about practicing his breathing. Okay, so maybe he didn't always get in a full fifteen minutes of practice twice a day; but he usually managed to squeeze in at least ten minutes. He also found that he could always work in several "mini-practice" sessions when he took his breaks at work. He practiced his breathing skills for two weeks before trying to use them when he was anxious. But it was hard for Tom to hold back. He wanted to try out this new anxiety management technique right away in a department meeting. Then he remembered how important it was to get some practice first in nonthreatening situations.

Once Tom felt that he had the hang of paced breathing, he gradually started using the skill whenever he felt his body reacting to fear. Once, in a meeting, his supervisor called on Tom to respond to a topic under discussion. He was able to take a few deep breaths before he answered. In fact, he was consciously aware of trying to breathe from his diaphragm, not his upper chest, as he spoke. Much to Tom's amazement, he didn't feel as shaky or sweaty as he usually did. He still worried about what others were thinking about him, but he felt some hope that at least he could manage some of his bodily symptoms.

Tom kept practicing and using his breathing skills whenever he could. He found that his anxiety level often fluctuated throughout the day. Sometimes it began to rise when he simply thought of an upcoming situation in which he would have to speak in public. By trial and error, he learned that the earlier he could implement his breathing skills, the better they worked. For example, as soon as he noticed his heart beating slightly fast, he would begin using the paced breathing technique. He was less successful when he ignored his body's early warning signs, and tried to use his skills when his anxiety level was already quite high.

Tom's situation illustrates several important points. First, like Tom, you may find that your anxiety level goes up and down throughout the day. That's normal. You shouldn't expect that using your breathing skills one time only will permanently reduce your anxiety level. Next, Tom found that his skills were most effective if he used them before his anxiety level became too high. The better he grew at noticing his early symptoms, the better he became at bringing his anxiety level down. Finally, you may find that it's difficult to be simultaneously anxious and breathing dia-phragmatically. This was the case for Tom. However, he still had trouble turning off his catastrophic thoughts, which were not only bothersome, but sometimes sabotaged his best effort to keep his anxiety level down. The skills in the next chapter helped Tom—and will help you—deal with this situation.

Handling Problems That May Occur

There are a couple of quick checks you can do if you're having dif-ficulty using paced breathing to bring your anxiety level down. Review this information and try out the suggestions that seem to best fit your situation.

You may be impatient for results. That's understandable. But it's im-possible to "hurry up and relax." You can't force it. In fact, trying to force yourself to breathe only increases the likelihood that you may hyperven-tilate. Give yourself both sufficient time for practice sessions and to master the skill.

Are you being consistent in your practice? You may get better results if you get into the habit of practicing at set times each day. Review your log. Are you really practicing as much as you think you are? Writing down your practice results will help you keep track of your practice ses-sions. Don't be surprised when you don't get good results if your practice is sporadic. Likewise, don't expect miracles overnight, especially if your practice isn't consistent. While a few weeks of practice should show re-sults, it may still be too early in your skill development for you to reduce your anxiety level when it's skyrocketing. It takes a good deal of practice to be able to reduce your symptoms at these moments of panic. As you continue to practice, you'll become better and better at decreasing your level of anxiety when it's at lower levels and in calming yourself after your anxiety peaks.

Review your comments section on the Anxiety Management Log. Are there constant interruptions or distractions that interfere with your practice? If so, what can you do about them? You may need to unplug the phone, or sit down with family members and let them know that you're not to be interrupted during the times you've set aside to practice.

Are you falling asleep during your practice sessions? Obviously, you can't get the full benefit of your practice if you keep falling asleep. You may need to change your location. Maybe lying on your bed is too big an invitation to nap. You may need to make yourself just a little less comfortable in order to keep awake. Changing your practice sessions to times when you're more alert may also help.

The comments section of your Log may reveal that you have bothersome thoughts or worries that crop up while you're practicing. If this is the case, try to avoid getting caught up in the thoughts. Acknowledge that a given thought is intruding on your practice, then shift your attention back to paced breathing. Again, we'll be discussing how to handle worrisome thoughts in the next chapter.

Despite your best efforts, you may find that instead of your anxiety decreasing while you're practicing, it increases. This phenomenon, called *relaxation-induced anxiety*, occurs in a small percentage of people who begin to practice anxiety management. It's the result of your body not being used to feeling relaxed. Instead, an alarm goes off indicating that something out of the ordinary is happening. In effect, your body is right. You're relaxing and experiencing a sensation that's quite unfamiliar. Although these sensations may be unsettling at first, the good news is that they go away. Don't lose heart as a result and avoid practicing your skills. Instead, keep at it. Relaxation-induced anxiety dissipates with continued practice of anxiety management skills.

Summary

In this chapter we laid the groundwork for mastering the skills necessary to overcome your social phobia. The first step involves managing your physical symptoms of acute anxiety. We presented one technique, paced breathing, that is effective in helping most people cope with anxious moments. In Chapter 12 we'll help you manage factors that may contribute to chronic and acute levels of anxiety.

6

Handling Your Mind's Reaction to Fear

Now that you've learned about your body's reaction to fear, we're going to ask you to take a look at the role your mind plays in the fear of disapproval. You probably remember from Chapter 1 that maladaptive thoughts are often part of anxiety. Chapter 2 mentioned unrealistic beliefs as a chief contributor to social phobias. In this chapter, we'll show you how maladaptive thoughts and unrealistic beliefs are related, and how they work against you. We'll also introduce a third concept—*inaccurate expectations*—and describe how these expectations make you exaggerate danger. Most importantly, we'll teach you strategies designed to change unwanted thoughts, beliefs, and expectations. These strategies are part of what is called cognitive therapy.

The Pioneers of Cognitive Therapy

In recent years, mental health professionals have become very aware of the strong influence our thoughts exert on our emotions and behavior. Psychologist Albert Ellis was one of the first to devise therapeutic techniques aimed at changing irrational cognitions that lead to unnecessary distress. His work in 1970 was followed by further theory and clinical strategies supported by a strong body of research. Contributions from psychologists Michael Mahoney in 1971 and Donald Meichenbaum in 1974 helped to build an impressive array of evidence that modifying your thoughts can truly lead to positive changes in feelings and actions. As was mentioned in Chapter 2, psychiatrist Aaron Beck showed in 1976 how the roots of depression can often be identified as irrational thoughts. Psychiatrist David Burns' ground-breaking 1980 self-help book, *Feeling Good: The New Mood Therapy*, spelled out how depression can be alleviated by substituting more realistic ways of thinking. Later, in 1985, Beck and his colleagues extended their methods in an effort to change thoughts that create or exacerbate anxiety. Burns' 1989 *The Feeling Good Handbook* described how people can use cognitive techniques for anxiety reduction on their own. Work by psychologist Richard Heimberg and his colleagues in 1985, by researchers Richard Mattick and Lorna Peters in 1988, and by others after them has specifically demonstrated that some of these ideas can be helpful in alleviating social phobias.

Understanding the Role of Thoughts, Beliefs, and Expectations

Before you learn about and change your own thoughts, beliefs, and expectations, it's important to understand how and when they are harmful. In particular, it is important to understand how the thoughts you experience in social situations can be maladaptive, how your basic beliefs about yourself and others may be unrealistic, and how your expectations about social danger may be inaccurate. These ideas are further explained below.

Maladaptive Thoughts

All individuals have an ongoing stream of thoughts running through their heads. Psychologists call these *automatic thoughts*: they just pop up, with little or no effort. These thoughts are automatic reactions to whatever situation you happen to be in at the time. Often, you're not even aware of them as you go about your routine business. Automatic thoughts are usually harmless or even pleasant. However, automatic thoughts that occur because of a phobia are maladaptive—they actually harm you in some way.

To give an example, imagine having just finished a conversation with an attractive person of the opposite sex. The thought comes into your head: "He (she) didn't like me. I didn't know what to talk about. I'm a loser." This string of thoughts related to a particular situation is bound to make similar situations difficult for you in the future. The situation becomes a trigger for the thoughts, and the thoughts are distracting—so distracting, in fact, that you may end up fulfilling your prophecy by not knowing what to say, by *acting* like a loser. For other examples of maladaptive thoughts, refer back to Chapter 1.

Unrealistic Beliefs

What causes maladaptive thoughts? They come from our basic belief systems. Most people hold a number of general but unrealistic beliefs that cause them to think maladaptively in certain situations.

Let's look at the above example again. What are the unrealistic beliefs underlying the thoughts, "He (she) didn't like me. I didn't know what to say"? The person experiencing these thoughts has a firmly held belief that goes something like this: "I'm a failure unless everyone likes me," or "I need to be perfect in order to be accepted by others." In contrast to thoughts that adjust and change from one interaction to the next, such beliefs are rigid: you carry them with you at all times; they serve as your general axioms or principles about people, the world, and yourself. Many if not most people are unaware of these core beliefs; but they can be uncovered if you take the time. It may be helpful first to review some of the more common unrealistic beliefs that can contribute to social phobia.

- If I'm anxious, I can't function around people.

- If I make one mistake, other people won't like me.

- If others think I'm no good, then it must be true.

- If I display any anxiety, others will judge me as weak.

- If I'm criticized for one specific thing, it's a criticism of my overall worth as a person.

- If others really knew me, they'd recognize me as an "imposter."

- If others disapprove of me, I won't be able to tolerate it.

This list is not exhaustive. You will learn how to discover other beliefs you may have that contribute to your social fears. Notice that many of these unrealistic beliefs tend to be perfectionistic and contain the idea that you should avoid disapproval. The section below offers tips on how to fight perfectionism and live with the inevitability of disapproval.

A Highlight on Perfectionism: How To Fight It

Perfectionsim is a common problem for people with social phobia. The perfectionist tends to set unrealistic and unattainable goals. Many people with social phobias feel that they can never make a mistake in front of others; in other words, they must be perfect. Obviously, such people can never feel satisfied with themselves until their belief in perfectionism changes.

Remember Tom, the police officer with the public-speaking phobia? Tom suffered from the core belief that he had to be perfect. Here is an example of his thought-monitoring process. Later in this chapter, you'll be learning to monitor your own thinking process.

Situation	Thoughts
Stumbled over words while talking at a meeting	I screwed up again! I should be able to make a simple statement without stumbling over my words.

This type of thinking exemplifies the perfectionism that can really exacerbate a social phobic's anxiety. Instead of feeling pleased that he got up the courage to make a comment, Tom is putting himself down for not being perfect.

Tom had to devote a fair amount of effort to overcoming his perfectionism. This is described further in the section on "mistake practice" in Chapter 9, which focuses on Tom's actions to correct this problem. Equally important, however, was Tom's willingness to try to think differently. He had to consider adopting a different attitude. As an alternative to his perfectionism, he tried saying to himself, "It's okay if I stumble over my words. I don't need to be perfect. I won't expect that of myself any longer."

Tom considered what he might have to gain by clinging to his old perfectionism, the belief that he's only acceptable if he does things flawlessly. He came to the conclusion that choosing to hold such a belief amounted to choosing unhappiness and constant dissatisfaction. After all, reasoned Tom, perfectionism is unattainable. Alternatively, more constructive ways of thinking lead to more positive feelings and significantly less anxiety.

Are you a perfectionist?

A Highlight on Living with Disapproval

Many people with social phobias believe that they have to be liked and approved of by everyone. They feel unable to handle rejection. Perhaps you share this view. If so, you will need to hear this message over and over again.

It's okay if some people dislike you or disapprove of you sometimes. In fact, it's inevitable.

Does this sound shocking or totally wrong to you? Unfortunately, many people are raised to believe that approval from everyone in every circumstance is a necessity. The problem with taking that attitude is that you are doomed to feel bad—because absolutely no one is liked by all, or has all their actions met with universal approval. Being liked is nice. Having the approval of others is terrific. However, these things aren't always essential, nor do they signify whether or not you are a good or a worthy person. You need only look around you (or back through history) to see that anyone's popularity or "approval rating" fluctuates over time and is never universal. Jesus and many other religious figures were both greatly loved and greatly hated. Van Gogh never sold a painting in his lifetime, but is regarded as an undisputed genius now. Did the actual worth of these people fluctuate? No, of course not. It's people's value judgments and opinions that have vacillated over time. If you judge yourself by what other people think, you will invariably lose.

It's really true that you can't please all of the people all of the time. It's not possible, and it's not necessary. Accepting that others will occasionally disapprove of you or react negatively can be an effective antidote for social phobia.

Do you see how such beliefs make you much more likely to experience maladaptive thoughts in social situations? Is it clear to you in what ways these beliefs are unrealistic? If so, then you are well on your way toward understanding how your mind influences your social phobia. If you're unconvinced, read on anyway.

Inaccurate Expectations

There's another piece to understanding this puzzle—that is, learning how your underlying, unrealistic beliefs can lead you to exaggerate "social danger," thus keeping your social phobia going. Your beliefs strongly influence your expectations of what will occur in a given situation. Realistic beliefs lead to accurate expectations. Unrealistic beliefs lead to overestimations of the danger of social situations.

There are two ways in which you can exaggerate the threat posed by a social situation. The first involves exaggerating the chances of disapproval occurring; the second involves exaggerating the consequences of what would happen if disapproval did occur. In other words, socially anxious folks tend to expect disapproval when it's not likely, and overestimate how bad disapproval will be if it actually occurs. They see disapproval as both highly probable and highly severe. These are called probability and severity distortions, because they make people exaggerate the probability and severity of disapproval. Probability and severity distortions lead to upsetting (and, as you'll eventually prove to yourself, ultimately inaccurate) conclusions that send social anxiety soaring. By seeing how these distortions make you exaggerate social danger, you can come to understand exactly how unrealistic some of your beliefs are. We will help you evaluate your own estimates of probability and severity later in this chapter.

The Relationship Between Thoughts, Beliefs, and Expectations

You now have a basic understanding of maladaptive thoughts, unrealistic beliefs, and inaccurate expectations. But you may still be unclear how these three concepts fit together. A look at the diagram below may be helpful.

Beliefs are the general principles and assumptions that guide you through life. They represent judgments about yourself and people in general. Your general beliefs influence what you expect to happen in each specific situation you encounter. If your beliefs are unrealistic, your expectations will be inaccurate. In the case of social phobia, unrealistic beliefs lead you to expect more danger than there actually is. When you enter a social situation falsely expecting danger, the thoughts you experience will be maladaptive—that is, they will make you feel uncomfortable unnecessarily and distract your attention from the task at hand. Remember, unrealistic beliefs lead to inaccurate expectations, which lead to maladaptive thoughts.

The Mental Components of a Social Phobia

Unrealistic Beliefs
(about yourself and others)

e.g., "If I display any anxiety, others will think I'm weak. I am incapable of tolerating other people's disapproval."

↓

Inaccurate Expectations
(about a specific situation)

e.g., "The audience will definitely see my anxiety during my speech tonight and it will be a total catastrophe."

↓

Maladaptive Thoughts
(while in the situation)

e.g., "The audience can see I'm anxious. They all hate me. My career is over."

Learning About Your Own Thoughts, Beliefs, and Expectations

Now that you have a basic understanding of how your mind's reaction to fear can keep your social phobia going, let's look at what you can do to break the cycle. How do you develop new thoughts, beliefs, and expectations? Well, before you can change them, you have to learn to recognize and identify them.

Identifying Your Maladaptive Thoughts

In order to identify your maladaptive thoughts, it is often necessary to monitor and record what goes on in your mind. For some readers, this may present itself as a relatively easy task; but others may be dubious. "How do I know what I'm thinking? I'm just anxious."

Let us assure you that even if spelling out your thoughts does not come naturally to you, most people can learn to do it. As with most skills, effort and practice will make a big difference. If you stick with it, you should quickly notice yourself becoming more aware of the constant stream of "self-talk" that goes on inside your head. The most necessary ingredient is simply a willingness to take the time to focus on your thoughts. This can be a challenge when you're busy and caught up in the ongoing surge of events that make up a single day. Nonetheless, developing the skill of thought monitoring can yield one of your most powerful tools for conquering social phobia.

It's not productive to look back days or weeks after an anxiety-provoking incident and ask yourself, "What was I thinking?" This may give you a bit of worthwhile information, but chances are good that you've forgotten many crucial details. So much more can be gleaned from a written thought record kept on a daily basis. On the next page is a form that you can use to "catch yourself in the act" of having maladaptive thoughts. Many people seen in our clinic have found this form extremely useful. Make several photocopies of the form, and always keep your current form with you. Make sure that you always carry something to write with, too! Use as much space as you need for each entry.

The thought diary requires you to rate your anxiety in the first column, using the 0-10 scale for anxiety described in Chapter 5. Make an entry whenever you are feeling anxious about a social situation. Note the date and time in the second column; then identify the situation briefly (for example, "Restaurant date with Mark"). In the fourth column, record an uncensored version of the thoughts that immediately run through your head (extending the previous example, "I'm going to make a fool of myself! This is going to be our first and last date. What a dope I was for ever saying yes!"). Fill out copies of this form over several days, both workdays and weekends. If you can't mark the form at the precise time when you're feeling socially anxious, just try and get back to it as soon as you can. The ideal is to write while your thoughts are reasonably fresh. This may seem like lots of work, but it's the best way to reveal the stream of self-talk that goes on in your head.

Thought Diary

Anxiety Level (0-10)	Date & Time	Situation	Maladaptive Thoughts
_____	_____	_____	_____
_____	_____	_____	_____
_____	_____	_____	_____
_____	_____	_____	_____
_____	_____	_____	_____
_____	_____	_____	_____
_____	_____	_____	_____
_____	_____	_____	_____
_____	_____	_____	_____
_____	_____	_____	_____
_____	_____	_____	_____
_____	_____	_____	_____
_____	_____	_____	_____
_____	_____	_____	_____
_____	_____	_____	_____
_____	_____	_____	_____
_____	_____	_____	_____
_____	_____	_____	_____
_____	_____	_____	_____
_____	_____	_____	_____
_____	_____	_____	_____
_____	_____	_____	_____

Identifying Your Unrealistic Beliefs

Okay, let's assume that you've made an all-out effort to monitor and record your thoughts. You now have an idea of the types of thoughts you experience when you're in, or when you're thinking about, feared social situations. The next step is to determine your beliefs.

Look at the list of unrealistic beliefs at the beginning of this chapter. Take a minute to think about whether any of these beliefs ring a bell. For instance, do you believe that if you're criticized for one specific thing, it's a criticism of your overall worth as a person? Do you believe that if others disapprove of you, you won't be able to tolerate it? If you're unsure, bear in mind that people are not always consciously aware of their beliefs. It may help to look back at the thought diary you completed in the previous section. As you read over your maladaptive thoughts, see if they provide any clues to the unrealistic beliefs you hold. Remember that you should check whether any of these beliefs *feel* correct to you, even if you understand intellectually that they're unrealistic. Use the space below to list any unrealistic beliefs that you're able to uncover.

My Unrealistic Beliefs

_____

_____

_____

_____

_____

Identifying Your Inaccurate Expectations

Let's take a look at your expectations about social danger, expectations that come from the unrealistic beliefs you just identified. Pick out a social situation from your thought diary that caused you particular anxiety. Write a brief description of that situation in the space below.

_____

_____

Next, think about your sense of how likely you were in that situation to experience disapproval. Using the first scale below, choose the percentage between 0 and 100 that best represents your sense of your chances for experiencing disapproval in that situation. Let your fear do the talking as you make the rating. What's important is how you actually felt, not

what you now think you should have felt. Write the percentage here:
_____.

My Chances for Experiencing Disapproval

0%	10%	20%	30%	40%	50%	60%	70%	80%	90%	100%

No chance of disapproval	Some chance		Fifty-fifty chance	Good chance		Definite disapproval

Now let's take a look at how you assess the severity of disapproval in that same situation. This time, what's important is how bad you felt it would have been if someone had disapproved of you or your behavior. Using the scale below, choose the percentage between 0 and 100 that best represents how severe or catastrophic you felt the consequences would have been if someone had disapproved of you. Write the percentage here:
_____.

How Severe the Consequences of Disapproval Would Be

0%	10%	20%	30%	40%	50%	60%	70%	80%	90%	100%

No problem whatsoever	Somewhat distressing		Severe	Very severe		The worst possible catastrophe

You should now have an idea of what your original expectations were. Chances are that you felt the probability of disapproval to be high, and the consequences of disapproval to be very severe ("I couldn't tolerate it," "Everyone would think I'm nuts," "I could never face them again," and so on). Since you've had these expectations for some time, you may feel that they're accurate. But don't be too sure. See what you discover when you evaluate the accuracy of your expectations in the next section.

Changing Your Thoughts, Beliefs, and Expectations

By now you probably have a better understanding of the types of maladaptive thoughts you experience in social situations, what your expectations are regarding the probability and severity of disapproval, and have identified your unrealistic beliefs that influence those thoughts and expectations. It's now time to develop healthier ways to think about and respond to social situations you fear. This involves developing more realistic beliefs and more accurate expectations. It also involves changing the way you think.

Replacing Maladaptive Thoughts with Coping Statements

To get rid of self-defeating thoughts like the ones you identified in your thought diary, you must learn to replace them with more adaptive and constructive thoughts, called *coping statements.*

What are some of the characteristics of a useful coping statement? First, it should be in your own words, not in language that seems abstract or removed from your problems. Second, it should apply directly to your particular concerns: if you worry about blushing, a coping statement about sweating just won't do. Third, a good coping statement should be realistic. Occasionally, we find someone trying to counter frightening thoughts with such statements as, "I'm not going to get real anxious," or, "I will be calm—I definitely won't say anything stupid." Such statements don't work well because they are unrealistic: you can't expect to completely control or eliminate anxiety. Further, notice how the coping statement, "I won't say anything stupid," has the anxious person promising to be perfect. Maybe he or she will make a remark that's a little foolish; such things happen. The statement would be better if it reminded the anxious person that it's okay to be human, that everyone has awkward moments—it's not a calamity.

Finally, coping statements should be relatively brief and simple. Keeping them short and to the point makes them easy to remember and use. This is important, because you will need to memorize your coping statement to make it truly useful.

Try writing your own coping statement now. Generally, many coping statements can be fit into the following format:

Most people will accept it if [what you fear happens].

I can cope with disapproval. It's not that bad.

Here are some examples that tie in with common goals you may be working on:

- Most people will accept it if my hands shake while I'm eating. I can cope with disapproval. It's not that bad.

- Most people will accept it if I stumble when giving a presentation.
  I can cope with disapproval. It's not that bad.

- Most people will accept it if I take a long time in the bathroom. I can cope with disapproval. It's not that bad.

- Most people will accept it if my handwriting is a little messy. I can cope with disapproval. It's not that bad.

- Most people will accept it if I say something silly on a date. I can cope with disapproval. It's not that bad.

Notice how these coping statements refute both probability and severity exaggerations. The first sentence reminds you that the probability of disapproval is lower than your fear says it is. The second sentence reminds you that you are capable of dealing with disapproval, and that the consequences of disapproval are not as severe as your fear would lead you to believe.

Write your coping statement here for future reference:

Most people will accept it if _____.

I can cope with disapproval. It's not that bad.

Now that you have your coping statement written, how do you actually put it to use? There are several ways. You can repeat your coping statement to yourself when you feel anxious. This serves to interrupt your maladaptive thoughts. (It's difficult to think of two different things at the same time!) In addition, repeating your coping statement offers you a healthier interpretation of the situation, thus attacking those unrealistic beliefs. Some people also like to use their coping statement along with their paced breathing skills. For example, instead of counting, you can repeat your coping statement each time you inhale and exhale. If you do this, be sure and practice timing your statements with your breathing, finding a rhythm that feels comfortable.

Some of you may have the reaction, "It's all very well to rehearse coping statements when you're calm, but I just know when that anxiety hits I won't be able to think straight." It's true that reassuring thoughts can be hard to summon as you get closer to the actual fear-inducing situation. That's why composing a brief, to-the-point coping statement, and memorizing that statement, is so important. You should know your coping statement so well that you can retrieve it instantly, without hesitation. It's essential to practice saying your coping statement to yourself on a daily basis.

You may also want to create and carry what we call a *coping card*. This is an index card with a series of coping statements written on it. The card gives you space to elaborate on and personalize your basic coping statement by adding other helpful comments that would be difficult to memorize. Although the coping card is a simple idea, many folks we work with swear by it. They have been able to discreetly review their card for a little "coping refresher course" just before giving a talk, or approaching someone attractive, or walking into a restaurant or public bathroom. Some people even find that having the coping card handy is calming whether they need to look at it or not. In our view, it's definitely worthwhile to carry it, especially when a difficult situation is coming up and anticipatory anxiety is likely. Of course, a coping card should not become a distraction. Instead, it should prepare you to focus on what you're experiencing and how to handle it.

Let's take a look at what Tom wrote on his coping card. His basic coping statement was, "Most people will accept it if I make a mistake during my speech. I can cope with disapproval. It's not that bad." Here's what his coping card looked like.

Coping Card

When a situation comes up in which I have to speak in public, chances are I'll be anxious. My heart will race and I'll probably sweat. Still, I can do my best even if I am real nervous—I can get through it. I just need to remember that the anxiety is uncomfortable, but it will pass soon. It's not important to be perfect—I'm human like everybody else. I will feel proud of having the guts to face this. When I face up to my fears, that helps me get over them. Most of all, I will remember that any kind of disaster is unlikely. Even if I do run into some disapproval, it's not the end of the world. The people I care about most will love me even if I don't make a smooth speech. I'll use my paced breathing to help the symptoms pass more quickly.

Your coping card may be very similar to Tom's, or it can be completely different. The important thing is that the statements on your card reassure you in a realistic way. Try and include refutations of exaggerated estimates of probability and severity, as well as logical comebacks to as many maladaptive thoughts as you can identify. Remember, though—while your coping card can contain quite a bit of positive self-talk, you still need a brief coping statement for those times when it's not practical or convenient to look at your card.

Developing More Accurate Expectations

Although it's important to be able to interrupt maladaptive thoughts, a lasting recovery requires adopting more accurate expectations about social situations.

We are going to ask you to reevaluate the probability and severity estimates of disapproval you made earlier in the chapter. You see, one of the reasons why people with a social phobia keep exaggerating the threat of danger is that they ignore information that contradicts their inaccurate expectations.

Start out by reconsidering your probability expectation—your estimate of how likely it was that disapproval would actually occur. (Refer to the situation you selected from your thought diary.) The idea is to see if you can develop a more accurate estimate of the probability that disapproval would occur in a similar situation. We've listed some ways to gather information that you might find helpful.

Ask other people. Pick people you feel comfortable approaching but who do not share your social fears. Describe the situation to them, and the consequences you fear (*My hand would shake, I'd blush, I'd forget my lines,* and so on). Then ask them what they might think if they witnessed this consequence. Would they disapprove of someone who blushed, stuttered, or forgot their lines? If their views are more charitable than what you expected, ask them why they would not disapprove. Try to determine how they are interpreting the situation differently than you would.

Examine your own experiences. Think as objectively as you can about the real evidence you have for your expectations. Ask yourself, "How many times have I been in that situation? How many times was there irrefutable evidence that other people disapproved of me?"

Consider the validity of the disapproval. In other words, on what basis would someone disapprove of you? What is so unacceptable about the consequences that would merit disapproval? Would your symptoms or behavior really justify the negative reactions of others?

Look for the influence of unrealistic beliefs. Review the unrealistic beliefs you wrote down earlier in this chapter. Is it possible that these beliefs might have led you to exaggerate the probability of disapproval?

After having considered the above questions, has your estimate of the probability of disapproval changed?

Let's follow a similar procedure to reevaluate your expectations about the severity of the consequences of disapproval. Earlier in this chapter, you gave a percentage rating to the severity of consequences in this situation. To help reevaluate this rating, consider the questions below.

Ask other people. This time, ask people about the severity of disapproval. How serious a matter would they consider it to be if they actually did disapprove of something someone else did in a social situation? If someone else disapproved of them in a similar situation, how important would they consider that to be? Do they think they could handle it? If they disapproved of someone else in a given situation, would their opinion of that person remain fixed, or would it be subject to reevaluation and change?

Examine your own experiences. Can you recall a time when you actually experienced disapproval? How did you feel? Did you stay in the situation to find out whether you really could handle it, or did you leave? If you did stay, how did you handle it? Did the disapproval last when you stayed? If you left, did the disapproval remain forever fixed?

Consider the validity of your assessment of severity. Is there a valid reason why someone would become very upset with you if your worst fears came true in a social situation? If so, is there a reason to expect you would not survive the experience? Do you think you would eventually see the unreasonableness of the other person's response? Does another person's opinion of you actually change you, your worth, or your life in any meaningful way?

Look for the influence of unrealistic beliefs. Again, review your list of unrealistic beliefs. Are any of these beliefs leading you to exaggerate the severity of the consequences of disapproval?

After considering whatever new information you have generated by following the procedures outlined above, develop a new severity estimate. Refer to the earlier scale ("How Severe the Consequences of Disapproval Would Be"), and choose the percentage that best represents your revised assessment. Is the percentage lower than your original expectation?

Developing More Realistic Beliefs

Perhaps at this point you are thinking, "Fine, I can say my coping statement and adjust my expectations, but I'm still stuck with the same old beliefs that keep getting me into trouble." It's true that changing beliefs usually takes longer than changing thoughts and expectations. It's hard to discard beliefs, unrealistic or not, that have been with you for a long time and have comprised such a basic part of how you think and feel about the world. Nonetheless, even the most stubborn belief can change under the right conditions. Be patient. As you change your expectations in various social situations, the false nature of some of your old beliefs will begin to become apparent. After all, those unrealistic beliefs are what made you exaggerate social danger in the first place. Perhaps you found yourself already questioning your beliefs as you changed the probability and severity estimates in the preceding section.

The most powerful way to change your beliefs is yet to come. This is only the beginning. In the next section of the book, you will learn a proven technique, called *exposure*, that will really put your thinking to the test. You'll be able to see for yourself which thoughts—your old maladaptive ones or your new coping statements—enable you to feel and perform better in social situations. You will be able to see first-hand whether your beliefs are realistic and whether your expectations are accurate.

Before you proceed though, it may help to see someone else's process of changing their thoughts, beliefs, and expectations.

A Practice Example

Tracy, 26, had a rather severe generalized social phobia. She felt very anxious conversing even briefly with anyone but her husband, other immediate family members, and a close friend or two. In her work as a salesperson at a department store, she was able to smile and be somewhat friendly. However, when the situation was purely social, Tracy felt completely inadequate. Consequently, she shunned any kind of party or social outing, avoiding almost everyone but her spouse. Tracy's anxiety about meeting people she'd be forced to interact with socially was so great that she avoided local restaurants, shopping malls, and movie theaters, often going many miles out of her way. She also missed out on a good deal of family life and friendship because of her fears.

How did Tracy go about the process of changing her thoughts, beliefs, and expectations? First, she set out to identify her maladaptive thoughts. Her thought diary certainly contained lots of clues about the roots of her fears. Here's an excerpt.

Date	Anxiety Level	Time	Situation	Maladaptive Thoughts
Mon.	6	5 p.m.	Invitation to sister's baby shower	I hate to disappoint Paula, but I just can't go. There will be at least 15 women there I'll have to relate to, and it'll be so awkward! I won't know whether to talk to them or what to say. When I do try to talk in that kind of situation, whatever I say sounds so boring and inane. Everyone will notice that I'm sweating and nervous. They'll feel sorry for Paula for having such a weirdo for a sister.

Do Tracy's thoughts seem familiar? It's often easier to see distortions in someone else's thinking than in your own. Take a closer look at Tracy's thoughts to see how they are maladaptive. In what ways are they likely to make her feel anxious and interfere with her ability to interact with others?

After identifying some of her maladaptive thoughts, Tracy examined the list of unrealistic beliefs commonly held by people with a social phobia. She discovered that several of them applied to her:

- If I display any anxiety, others will judge me as weak.

- If I make one mistake, other people won't like me.

- If others disapprove of me, I won't be able to tolerate it.

Tracy was also able to identify and jot down some of her other unrealistic beliefs that underpinned her fears:

- No one wants to be associated with such a neurotic—my parents and my sister must be ashamed of me.

- The other guests will think I'm weird or even crazy if they notice how anxious I am. I'm going to be the only one there feeling nervous and awkward.

- People who have symptoms like mine are socially unacceptable. If I go to the baby shower, I'm going to be faced with devastating rejection. People will wonder if craziness runs in our family.

- It's very important for people to react positively to everything I do. My worth as a person depends on other people's acceptance and approval.

After confronting her beliefs in black and white, Tracy could see how they might be judged unrealistic, especially by an outsider. Yet, she knew that these beliefs reflected how she truly felt.

Her next step was to look carefully at how her beliefs shaped her expectations and determined her tendency to exaggerate the threat of social harm. She had already estimated the probability of experiencing disapproval if she attended her sister's baby shower. Using the same scale you used, she identified a 95 percent probability that what she had to say would be perceived as boring and inane, and that other people would notice her anxiety. Now she prepared herself for the task of reevaluating this expectation. She began by mustering the courage to talk with a friend about what her reaction would be if Tracy said something boring at the baby shower. The friend told Tracy that she found their conversations to be generally interesting; she asked Tracy how she arrived at such a negative judgment about her communication skills. What kinds of things did she fear she might say that would be judged so harshly?

Confiding in her friend, Tracy said that she would probably start out with "How are you?" if she had met the person before, and perhaps comment on how excited she was at the prospect of becoming an aunt. Her friend shrugged her shoulders and pointed out that these remarks seemed perfectly pleasant and appropriate, even if they were hardly earthshaking. She asked if Tracy would consider such remarks boring and inane if they came from someone else. Tracy acknowledged that she wouldn't think negatively at all about another person opening a conversation with such pleasantries.

Talking with her friend helped Tracy begin to see things in a new light. She reviewed her prior experience and had to admit that she could not recall many instances in which there were clear signs that other people found her boring. She then asked herself, "Even if I say something boring, is it valid for someone else to disapprove of me as a person because of this?" She was able to see how unlikely it was for someone to disapprove of her in general because she was temporarily unengaging. Perhaps, she acknowledged, her low self-confidence was leading her to judge herself—and others—too harshly. In light of this, and after consideration, she altered her estimate of the probability that her comments would be seen as boring and inane to 30 percent—quite a change! Tracy thought, "I *feel* boring and inept in those situations, but I guess that doesn't mean that I'm necessarily coming across that way." This, too, was an important realization: bad feelings about yourself aren't necessarily based on fact. Plenty of nice folks with lots to be proud of walk around with a poor self-image. If you catch yourself in the act of giving yourself a negative label, ask yourself if you're being reasonable. Chances are that your negative feelings about yourself are exaggerated.

Tracy went on to reexamine her estimate of the probability that others would notice that she was sweating and anxious. She had given this a 100 percent probability. Does this number seem reasonable to you? Tracy considered some evidence she had previously overlooked; then acknowledged that others had commented that she looked anxious only a few times out of the multitude of occasions when she had been perspiring and very nervous. She was also able to remember how surprised her husband and family had been to learn of the extent of her social fears. They had even remarked that, although she seemed rather quiet and withdrawn, she seldom came across as obviously anxious! Yet another bit of evidence that led her to revise her probability estimate came from her observation of others. Tracy was able to see that other people are sometimes nervous without overtly displaying anxiety. For example, she recalled attending a fellow staff member's smooth presentation at a meeting, and her surprise to later hear the staff member describe how frightened she had felt giving the presentation.

After reviewing these and other bits of evidence, Tracy revised her estimate of the chances of others noticing her anxiety to 25 percent. She realized that she had been assuming that people were always paying close attention to her every word and action. Like many others with social phobias, she forgot that people might have more on their minds than the task of analyzing and judging her. Tracy's new, more adaptive thought was, "Someone might notice my nervousness, but chances are that they won't." Obviously, this more realistic thought made it a bit easier to contemplate going to the baby shower.

Did Tracy exaggerate the severity of the consequences of disapproval as well? This was one of her thoughts on the subject: "Maybe there's only a small chance that other people will find me boring and inane, or that they'll notice my anxiety," she reasoned, "but if they did find me that way it would be unbearable." Tracy felt that the world would end if others disapproved of her. To her, this was an absolute catastrophe worthy of a 90 on the severity scale. She felt that it would create a family disaster if she said something boring or if others noticed and disapproved of her anxiety. In her mind, her relationship with her sister, the love and approval of her parents, even the health of the baby all hinged on Tracy's ability to perform well in a tricky social situation. When you consider some of Tracy's unrealistic beliefs, it's not surprising that she would perceive disapproval as so catastrophic.

In the process of reevaluating this expectation, Tracy talked with her friend again, who did not share Tracy's excessive concern about being approved of by others, and felt that any negative reactions would quickly pass. When thinking of the few instances in which someone did express disapproval of her, Tracy remembered that these situations were uncomfortable, but not catastrophic, and temporary rather than permanent. She also could see that an extreme reaction of disapproval would be an inappropriate response to an uninteresting comment or evidence of perspiration. Tracy was also able to challenge her idea that it would be a terrible thing if others disapproved of her. "I could learn to live with it," she told herself. "Their opinions do not change who I am." She revised her estimate of the severity of the consequences of disapproval to 50 percent.

Tracy began to realize that no one is liked universally. Why should she expect to be the great exception to the rule, that everyone should like her? Did she feel positive toward each person she met? Of course not. There are many ways in which people differ; she tended to gravitate toward certain people, and to feel less drawn to others. Reasons for liking or not liking often have much more to do with one's own past and personal associations than with the other person's attributes, accomplishments, or behavior. In other words, liking or disliking, approval or disapproval, are largely personal, subjective phenomena.

"Why is it essential that everyone like you, anyway?" Tracy asked herself. "You certainly don't have time to be friends with the entire local population. Anyway, it's practically impossible to win some people's approval due to *their* negative characteristics. Certain people are insensitive and unkind, and generally unaccepting (or you may remind them of their old college roommate with whom they had a tremendous falling out ten years ago). It's just not worth upsetting yourself if someone frowns on your behavior, your taste, your clothes, your sense of humor: you're never going to please everyone! So you might as well just focus on pleasing yourself."

For most people, cultivating a few close relationships, rather than the adulation of the masses, makes life rewarding and fulfilling. It's just a fact—even the most popular, brilliant, gorgeous human beings in the world get rejected sometimes. That's life. Problems arise when people attach too much meaning and importance to the inevitable rejections that life brings. Rejection can be very disappointing. It can really hurt. But it doesn't have to devastate you. It's really not a catastrophe unless you make it one.

Taking all of this into account, Tracy was able to modify her expectations of what might happen at the baby shower. She began to reevaluate her unrealistic beliefs about disapproval in general. In addition, she developed a useful coping statement: "Most people will accept it if I say something boring or if I show signs of anxiety. And I can cope with disapproval. It's not that bad."

Summary

In this chapter, we looked at the role that maladaptive thoughts and unrealistic beliefs play in creating and increasing social anxiety. We described how someone with a social phobia exaggerates the probability and severity of social danger, and how these inaccurate expectations lead to fear. In addition, we showed you how to identify your maladaptive thoughts, and how to replace them with a healthier coping statement. We also gave you a method for changing your old beliefs and expectations to help you gain a new perspective. These tools, along with the paced breathing skills you learned in Chapter 5, will help you in the chapters ahead as you learn to face your fear of disapproval.

Recommended Reading

Burns, D. (1989) *The Feeling Good Handbook*. New York: Williams Morrow & Company.

SECTION IV

Facing Your Fear of Disapproval

In this section we explain the central behavioral technique for combating social phobia—exposure. Chapter 7 defines exposure and explains the rationale behind it; Chapter 8 helps you list the particular exposures that you will need to do. Chapter 9 gives you in-depth case examples of exposure treatment, and Chapter 10 provides guidelines for making this technique maximally effective.

7

Exposure: A Method for Facing Your Fears

By now you have prepared yourself for actually making important behavior changes. You've planned, set goals, learned needed skills, and begun to alter unhealthy thinking styles. It's time for action!

Exposure—How It Works for You

The basic tool you will use in taking action to combat your social fears is a technique called *exposure*. The term exposure simply refers to the process of facing your fears, rather than avoiding situations that engender them. If you are like most socially anxious people, you have become an expert in avoiding the situations that bring on anxiety symptoms. No one enjoys feeling scared and upset. Naturally, then, people tend to keep their distance from interactions that make them uncomfortable. You may even avoid thinking about difficult social situations.

It is important to understand the principle of how exposure works. Unless you do, you may not follow through with your recovery plan. In order to enter frightening situations deliberately, you have to believe that it will pay off with results.

Essentially, exposure works in three ways. First, it helps you learn that certain actions will not lead to disapproval, or that when disapproval occurs it's not a catastrophe. In other words, exposure allows you to disprove and correct inaccurate beliefs. Second, repeated, graduated exposure allows you to become used to, or to *habituate* to, anxiety-provoking interactions. Third, properly planned and executed exposures build confidence that enables you to take the next step. We'll talk first about disproving and correcting maladaptive beliefs.

Disproving Maladaptive Beliefs

When you shun all interactions that entail addressing a group, you never learn that you can get through such situations without terrible consequences. As discussed in previous chapters, avoidance maintains maladaptive beliefs about the probability or severity of social "disasters" that an individual with social fears expects. When you avoid them, you have no opportunity to learn that you can function better than you expected in social circumstances, as many people have discovered with the help of exposure. Without exposure, you continue to believe that you'll look like a fool, or that you'll be criticized or disliked. Likewise, the person who dreads eating in public, and consistently avoids restaurants and group meals, never has the opportunity to see that he or she can finish a meal without a "disastrous" clumsy incident occurring. Catastrophic expectations can never be proven wrong when you avoid fear-provoking situations.

You may be thinking, "Hey! There are no guarantees that I can face my fears without a disaster resulting." This is certainly true. If you have had a traumatic social mishap in the past, it will be especially hard to face situations which you feel put you at risk for having a bad experience. However, in our clinical experience, the vast majority of exposures result in positive learning. (Of course, proper planning and skills training are essential to achieve these positive results.) People are often pleasantly surprised, even shocked, to find that a situation that they have dreaded for years was not so difficult after all. Moreover, there is relief in taking action, doing something positive to help yourself. Taking action helps you feel stronger, more in control, and, eventually, less fearful.

Most exposures are uncomfortable. They often provoke anxiety. In fact, they should—because you can't learn to cope with anxiety unless you experience it. Still, you learn that anxiety can't actually harm you, and that the nervous symptoms do eventually pass. You can endure temporary discomfort when it's pain with a purpose. You will find that in time you can become much more comfortable in social situations than you ever believed possible.

Habituation—How Your Body Calms Down

Beyond showing you that your fears were groundless or much exaggerated, exposure helps you in a second way. With repeated, properly executed exposures, your body begins to react more calmly in a situation that used to make you nervous. This occurs naturally (to some extent) with repetition. We call this *habituation*. Habituation means getting accustomed to certain things that once led to fear. To clarify: Can you think of a time when you've been startled by an unexpected loud noise? Perhaps a jackhammer or another noisy tool was being used for an un-scheduled repair just outside your normally quiet office. Your body and mind reacted to the noise. Very quickly, your heart rate increased, muscles grew tense, your breathing became more rapid and shallow. You wondered what in the world was going on.

If the noise became regular and repeated, and you understood and expected it, your body and mind would eventually stop responding so strongly, even if the noise continued to irk you a bit. Similarly, social in-teractions can lose their power to set off a strong anxiety response once they have become a more familiar, less threatening experience.

Confidence Building

There is a third payoff for completing exposures. When you face your fears and do what you have set out to do, your confidence grows. You build a store of successful experiences that you can refer to for in-spiration and reassurance. You are then more likely to face your fears the next time.

Types of Exposures

You might be thinking to yourself, "How can I just dive into a situation I've been avoiding for so long? Isn't there a way to ease into exposures?" The answer is yes. Chances are, you're feeling doubtful and scared as you consider facing your fears. Let us reassure you that, on the pages ahead, we'll help you carefully plan for these challenges, armed with the appropriate skills. Cognitive strategies and methods to reduce physiologi-cal symptoms are tremendously helpful in carrying out exposures. Above all, we recommend a gradual approach that makes exposures less threat-ening. We'll tell you how to work toward your goals in manageable steps.

There are two types of exposure: real-life or *in vivo* exposure and an intermediary step which we call *imaginal* exposure. With *in vivo* ex-posures, the socially-anxious person approaches the actual feared situa-tion, in real life. He or she walks into a public bathroom, gives a talk, eats in a restaurant, or chats with a co-worker who is normally avoided. These are essential and irreplaceable steps to overcoming social fears.

Imaginal exposure is what it sounds like—you face your fears by imagining social interactions that you avoid or dread. This type of ex-posure can be used to help prepare you for *in vivo* exposure; but there are other important uses for imaginal exposure as well. It's especially ef-fective if you have vivid, scary thoughts, or if your fear is so strong that *in vivo* exposure seems overwhelming. In the next several chapters, we'll show you how to integrate imaginal exposure into your recovery plan.

Summary

The basic technique you will use to overcome your fear of disapproval is called exposure. Exposure is the process of facing your fears. It works by disproving maladaptive beliefs about social disasters, helping your body become less reactive to social situations, and building confidence for future social encounters. There are two basic types of exposure—*in vivo* (direct) and imaginal. Now that you understand how this technique works, you're ready to design your own step-by-step exposures.

8

Ranking Your Fears: Creating an Exposure Hierarchy

The last several chapters have asked you to take a good, thorough look at your goals and objectives, and at your social fears. Additionally, they have spelled out some concrete skills and techniques you can use to manage anxiety. You have learned about exposure, the actual work of taking on a feared and previously avoided social situation. The next step is to make a detailed list of all the situations you associate with fear of disapproval, and rank them according to the degree of anxiety each evokes. We call this list your *exposure hierarchy*.

Coming Up with Hierarchy Items

Composing your hierarchy is a relatively straightforward task. The best place to begin is to refer back to your goal and list of objectives in Chapter 3. Take the objectives you wrote down and think of specific examples of each one. What particular situations do you want to enter? What do you want to do when you get there? Objectives are stated in general terms that let you know when you've achieved your goal; hierarchy items are much more concrete and detailed, describing specific behaviors in specific settings. Each description should be detailed enough so that if you were to go out and attempt an exposure right now, you'd know exactly where to go, what to do, with whom you'd be interacting, and so on.

Let's use the example of Tom again to see how this works. One of his objectives was, *I will accept invitations to give public education programs.* For his hierarchy, Tom needs to think of specific examples of the type of talks he wants to be able to give. This was relatively easy for him. All he had to do was think back over the years to all the times he had been asked to give presentations, but declined because of his social phobia.

Here's how Tom's objective looked when he expanded it for his exposure hierarchy:

- Speak to the fifth-grade class at St. William's School (parochial school) about crime prevention for about 30 minutes.

- Speak to tenth-grade class at Southwest High School (inner city school) about drugs and gangs for about 30 minutes.

- Talk to children at Northwest Plaza Mall about traffic safety during entire Saturday afternoon.

- Respond to local TV station's request for an on-camera interview about the increase in neighborhood crime.

Do you see how these are all very specific examples of his more general objective?

Now write down your own hierarchy items on the next page. Use extra paper if you need it. Don't censor yourself, or hesitate to jot down whatever ideas come to mind. Perhaps mastering some of these situations seems utterly impossible to you now; but write them down anyway. We're not asking for what you're sure you can learn to do, but what you really *want* to do. In our experience, people can overcome social fears they were certain would plague them always. For example, the thought of speaking before a television camera terrified Tom, yet he included the on-camera interview on his list.

Notice that each of Tom's hierarchy items is likely to bring on a different level of anxiety. Talking to a group of fifth graders about crime prevention seemed much more manageable to him than speaking to the news media. Don't worry at this point about precisely how much anxiety each exposure would bring on. Just compose your list of all possible examples of exposures that would pertain to your objectives. In the next section, we'll take on the task of ranking your feared situations by the amount of anxiety they evoke. Right now, just concentrate on putting down a complete list of exposure ideas for each objective you set in Chapter 3.

Of course, the length of the list will vary according to the extent of your social fears and avoidance. One person may have five situations to work on, another will have fifty. If you are closer to the latter, don't be disheartened. It may take a while to reach your goal; but we've seen many folks with a great deal of avoidance go just as far as those who were much less intimidated at the beginning of treatment.

Items To Include in My Hierarchy

_____

_____

_____

_____

_____

_____

_____

_____

_____

_____

_____

_____

Creating an Exposure Hierarchy

Now that you have a list including at least several items for each objective you set in Chapter 3, you're ready to create your actual hierarchy. This involves putting the items in order of difficulty according to how much anxiety they create for you. It's important to recognize at the outset how big a challenge an exposure represents, and to time it accordingly. You need to rank each specific situation in the hierarchy ahead of time, and to take on each as you are ready. This issue of timing exposures will be discussed at great length in the next few chapters. For now, you simply need to prepare your hierarchy by going back through your list of situations, and assigning each to the level of difficulty it represents.

How do you determine level of difficulty? Remember the 0-10 anxiety rating scale first introduced in Chapter 5, in which 0 represents no discomfort, on up through 10, which represents the worst anxiety you've ever endured? You'll be using the concept of this scale again to rate your hierarchy items. We've found that sometimes it's difficult to assign each item an exact number; so for this task we'll suggest a slight adaptation of the 0-10 scale. What you need to do is rate each item according to whether it would be a low-, medium-, or high-challenge exposure. A low-challenge exposure would be one that would likely elicit an anxiety level between 0-3, a medium-challenge exposure would probably bring on an anxiety level between 4-7, while a high-challenge exposure would peak your anxiety level at somewhere between 8-10.

Let's go through a brief example before we go on. Janice ended up with several items on her hierarchy list pertaining to one of her objectives, "I will attend parties." These hierarchy items included the following situations:

- Go to cousin's wedding shower, talk to at least two other guests.

- Go to cocktail party given by neighbors and stay half an hour.

- Attend office Christmas party without spouse and stay for two hours.

Now she needed to rank these as either low-, medium-, or high-challenge exposures. Janice felt that going to her cousin's wedding shower would be bearable. She was close to her cousin and would know several of the other guests. She estimated that her anxiety level would probably not be above a 3, so she ranked this as a low-challenge exposure. In contrast, the neighborhood cocktail party seemed quite threatening. She really didn't know any of her neighbors well, and she wasn't at all sure what she would talk with them about. She anticipated that her anxiety level would be between an 8 or 9 if she attended such a party, so she ranked this as a high-challenge exposure. The Christmas party fell somewhere in between. She knew her co-workers so that would make it a little easier, but her husband wouldn't be there, which would make it more difficult. She wasn't sure exactly where her anxiety level would fall for this one, but her best guess was that it would qualify as a medium-challenge exposure.

Of course, your experience in the actual exposure situation may turn out to be rather different; but almost everyone has a general sense of which social situations are hardest and which are easier. You can always correct your rankings later if you suspect that your initial expectation was off the mark. The hierarchy is not a one-shot deal with each item written in stone. Rather, it is a flexible list that you can reassess or add to as you move along towards achieving your goal.

Use the form provided here to make the first draft of your hierarchy. Write in pencil so that you can make changes if you need to. You can also refer to the examples below.

Some Hierarchy Examples

Let's take a closer look at a few examples to help you create your own hierarchy. Brenda, a 24-year-old executive secretary for a construction company, felt generally at ease in many social situations. Her job required her to talk on the phone and greet people as they came in the door, and she easily engaged in friendly small talk. She had several friends and dated from time to time. Brenda's social phobia was limited to very specific situations that involved eating or drinking in front of other

Exposure Hierarchy

Low-Challenge Exposures: Anxiety Level 0-3

_____

_____

_____

_____

_____

_____

_____

_____

_____

Medium-Challenge Exposures: Anxiety Level 4-7

_____

_____

_____

_____

_____

_____

_____

_____

_____

High-Challenge Exposures: Anxiety Level 8-10

_____

_____

_____

_____

_____

_____

_____

_____

people. She avoided such situations at all costs, which was beginning to limit her social life. It was hard to explain to her friends, much less a date, why she wouldn't do anything involving eating. Naturally, sometimes people didn't understand and thought she just wasn't interested in them. Her phobia also made her job less enjoyable, because she missed out on the socializing that naturally occurred during lunch and coffee breaks. As you can imagine, Brenda was eager to overcome her phobia so she could begin to enjoy a fuller social life. Let's look at her original recovery goal and her objectives, and see how she expanded them for her hierarchy.

Goal:

I want to eat and drink in public situations comfortably.

Objectives

- I will be able to eat and drink in restaurants.

- I will be able to eat and drink with co-workers.

- I will be able to invite others to my apartment for a meal.

Brenda's Exposure Hierarchy

Low-Challenge Exposures: Anxiety Level 0-3

Have a cup of coffee and donut with one co-worker on a break.

Have a few friends over to my apartment for pizza.

Go out for a snack after matinee movie with girlfriends.

_____

_____

_____

_____

Medium Challenge Exposures: Anxiety Level 4-7

Eat lunch at fast-food restaurant with girlfriends.

Eat lunch in staff kitchen with co-workers.

Attend a "happy hour" at Houlihan's restaurant and be able to eat and drink with friends.

Eat dinner with date at casual restaurant, like Two Nice Guys.

_____

_____

High Challenge Exposures: Anxiety Level 8-10

Eat dinner at fancy, expensive restaurant, like at the Ritz Carlton, with boss and other co-workers for annual employee appreciation awards ceremony.

Attend Sarah's wedding reception, sit-down dinner.

Accept invitation to an extended family holiday dinner.

Eat dinner with date at nice restaurant, like Chez Louis.

What about Tom? Let's look at his exposure hierarchy.

Tom's Exposure Hierarchy

Low-Challenge Exposures: Anxiety Level 0-3

Speak to fifth-graders at St. William's School (parochial school) about crime prevention for 30 minutes.

Say grace in front of immediate family on Friday night.

Talk to children at Northwest Plaza mall about traffic safety on a Saturday afternoon.

Ask question in department meeting.

Make comment in department meeting.

Greet people at door of church and hand out bulletins, 9:00 service

Medium-Challenge Exposures: Anxiety Level 4-7

Give presentation to tenth-grade students at Southwest High School (inner city school) on drugs and gangs for one hour.

Say grace at family gathering at Uncle Bob's, approximately 10 local relatives there.

Read a brief announcement at church, 10:30 service.

Express an opinion at a department meeting.

High Challenge Exposures: Anxiety Level 7-10

Speak on-camera to news media about increase in crime.

Say grace at large family reunion involving distant relatives from all across the country.

Give one of the scripture readings at 10:30 church service.

Give presentation to police officer colleagues on crisis management.

You're now ready to move on to Chapter 9 to see how to use your exposure hierarchy.

Summary

In this chapter we've taken you through the process of creating your own personal exposure hierarchy. Hierarchy items are specific, action-oriented expansions of the objectives you set in Chapter 3. The first step in devising your hierarchy is to jot down a list of social situations you want to master, and then rank-order them into three basic categories, depending on how much anxiety they evoke. In the next chapter, you'll learn the actual process of carrying out your exposures.

9

Carrying Out Your Exposures

In this section, we've discussed the three ways exposure works: by disproving inaccurate beliefs, allowing your body to habituate to anxiety-provoking interactions, and building your confidence. We mentioned the two basic types of exposure, *in vivo* and imaginal, and showed you how to rank the situations you fear by creating an exposure agenda. Now we'll take you step-by-step through the process of overcoming your social fears.

It can be difficult to know what type of exposure to do first. This section will help you decide where to start and how to proceed. To work your way through this chapter, you need to have your hierarchy completed and readily available. To start, review your list of low-challenge exposures and pick one that you'll work with throughout the six steps outlined below. Remember, it's important to start with a low-challenge item. Later you can work on more difficult situations. We'll use the example of Tom again to help illustrate how everything fits together.

Step 1: Imaginal Exposure

Facing social fears in imagination is often the logical place to begin. For some of you, starting off with real-life (*in vivo*) exposures can be overwhelming. Imaginal exposure helps prepare you for the next step, which is to experience your exposures in real-life situations. If you feel that you want to start off right away with *in vivo* you can skip to step 2, described in the next section. It isn't mandatory to start with imaginal exposure; but, still, it doesn't hurt to take your time and get some practice with the principle of exposure itself before plunging ahead with *in vivo* experience.

Here's how to begin. Read this section through to the end before you initiate your exposure.

First you'll want to find a quiet place where you won't be disturbed. Sit in a comfortable chair with your eyes closed. Use your breathing skills, or other techniques that work for you, and spend a few minutes relaxing. Then take the item you've selected from the low-challenge section of your hierarchy and imagine yourself entering that situation. Try to create the situation as clearly as you can using a tremendous amount of detail. Involve all your senses. What are you wearing? Are your surroundings hot, cold, humid, stuffy? What is the temperature of the air? Are you sweating? Can you breathe freely? What sounds can you hear? Can you hear traffic, the noise of copying machines, the sounds of people murmuring, the rustle of fabric, a water cooler bubbling? Can you hear your heart beating? Can you smell cigarette smoke, or disinfectant, or chlorine, or formaldehyde? Perhaps you can smell someone's perfume, or the smell of new carpets, or someone's sweat. How do your clothes feel on your body? If you imagine yourself seated, what is the texture of the furniture you're sitting on? If you're standing, what does the floor feel like beneath your feet? Is it carpeted? Is it hardwood, marble, linoleum, cement? Or are you standing outside on a grassy lawn? If you're about to drink from a glass, what is the temperature of the liquid? Is your mouth dry? Can you smell hors d'oeuvres? Doughnuts? Create as many details as you can concerning the people around you: the color and cut of their clothes, their posture, their expressions, the subtleties of their body language.

In addition to involving a tremendous amount of detail using all of your senses, your imaginal exposure should, in effect, tell a story. You should include a beginning (the actions leading up to the feared social situation), a middle (the actual social situation itself), and an end (any pertinent thoughts, feelings, or events that take place following the situation). When doing any kind of imaginal work, it is always an option to tape-record your description of the scene—then you'll have it available to listen to repeatedly. Some people jot down some notes ahead of time, or even write the entire script, before making the tape. Others are able to imagine the scene easily, without these preliminaries.

As you imagine the scene at length and in great detail, your anxiety level will rise. This is normal, and necessary for the exposure to work. Realize that you are going to feel uncomfortable, but that the discomfort will pass in time. Typically, your anxiety level will peak at a moderate level, then subside. If your anxiety rises to an overwhelming level, use the skills you've learned, such as deep breathing and coping statements, to calm yourself. But remember: the anxious feelings will not harm you, even if they are not particularly pleasant. You may also need to pick an easier item to begin your imaginal practice, and return to the more difficult scene as soon as you are ready. The basic idea is to keep imagining the scene, focusing on the particularly difficult portions, until your anxiety level drops noticeably. It's important not to switch your attention away from the scene until your mood improves; you need to learn that tolerating the image leads to eventual relief. What should happen is that each time you picture the scene, your anxiety level will be lower and lower. A general guideline is to repeat the scene (or the tape) as often as is necessary until your anxiety level drops to a 3 or less.

Using the form on the next page, keep a record of all of your imaginal exposure sessions. Note the date and the time and the exposure you're doing (for example, making a comment in a meeting). Keep track of your anxiety level in the next column. Also jot down any anxious thoughts you're aware of during your exposure. Then, later, you can use your cognitive coping skills to refute your maladaptive thoughts, as described in Chapter 6.

Let's see what Tom did with this step. The low-challenge item he selected was to make a brief comment during a department meeting. Tom had spent years going to meetings, never uttering a sound. He often had opinions about topics that were discussed, but was unable to speak his mind. In this first step, Tom followed the procedures described above—although finding a quiet place at home with three kids and a dog was quite a challenge!

Tom imagined in detail the room where department meetings were always held. He imagined his fellow officers and visualized the usual places where people sat, the clock on the wall, the window that looked across at another building. He imagined the stale odor of cigar smoke he could always smell in that room, and heard the ringing of telephones and murmur of voices from the main station room. Tom also imagined how he would feel, knowing that he was going to make a comment during the meeting. He concentrated on how his heart might beat rapidly and how he might even sweat a bit, especially just before he was about to speak. He imagined how he would feel scared and how he might even want to back out and not say anything after all.

Then Tom imagined actually making his comment. He didn't say anything earth-shattering or controversial at this point, just a fairly neutral comment that wouldn't be given a second thought. In his imaginary scene, Tom even stumbled over his words once, but continued. His fellow officers didn't die of shock when he actually said something. They even seemed interested. Tom systematically imagined the scene over and over again until he could do so with minimal anxiety before progressing to the next step.

The principle of habituation—even when experienced in his imagination alone—allowed Tom to reduce his troublesome symptoms of social phobia. He began to accustom himself to a situation he had avoided even thinking about in the past. Now that he could face this fear-producing situation in his mind, he was ready to use the same techniques of exposure in real life.

Weekly Exposure Log

Date/Time	Situation/ Exposure	Anxiety Level (0-10)	Anxious Thoughts During Exposure	Challenges or Coping Statements to Counteract Anxious Thoughts

Step 2: *In Vivo* Exposure

After mastering your fear in imagination, you're ready to face the feared social situation in real life. It can be difficult doing your first *in vivo* exposure—but don't turn back now! The rewards are worth the effort!

In most cases, the directions for *in vivo* exposure are the same as those for imaginal exposure. For example, for this step Tom makes a comment during an actual department meeting. Other situations may be harder to stage, especially those involving a one-time event (an audition for a particular play, a birthday party, a job interview). In such cases, you'll just have to rehearse in your imagination until the actual event comes up; or you may be able to adapt the exposure for a similar event (another audition, a different party, a job interview you don't really care about).

Here are the instructions for carrying out this step:

- Use the same low-challenge item from your hierarchy which you previously used for your imaginal exposure.

- Enter the situation and carry out the exposure (for example, go out on a date, eat in a restaurant, make a comment in a meeting).

- Your anxiety level will rise to a moderate level. This is a sign that the exposure is working. Allow yourself to feel the anxiety and realize that it won't harm you; that you can tolerate it.

- You can use your deep breathing and cognitive coping skills to keep your anxiety manageable. But, remember—you can't expect to eliminate anxiety.

- If you find that your anxiety level is higher than you expected when you first constructed your hierarchy, and you feel that things are getting out of control, it's okay on occasion to retreat from the situation. Perhaps you need to work on an easier item first. Return to the more difficult situation as soon as you feel ready.

- Keep a record of your exposure sessions. Be especially vigilant about monitoring your maladaptive thoughts during your exposures and constructing alternative ways of thinking.

Let's see how Tom did carrying out his exposure in real life. The morning of the department meeting, Tom's anxiety level was higher than usual in anticipation of the exposure, but he expected this. He knew that planning to speak in the department meeting was a new experience, and he wasn't discouraged when he felt a little uneasiness in his stomach. He took a few breaks in his morning routine to do some deep breathing. That helped calm him. He noticed his mind wandering ahead to the meeting, trying to imagine how it would go. He kept reminding himself that whatever happened, it would be a learning experience, and he would be able to feel proud of himself for taking the risk.

The meeting rolled around quickly and Tom walked to the usual room and took his usual seat. He was a bit disconcerted at first, because not everyone sat just where he imagined they would. (That's one reason why *in vivo* exposures can be a bit tougher—you don't have the same kind of control as you do in your imagination.) The meeting began and various topics were discussed. Tom kept passing up opportunities to say something, waiting for the "perfect" time. Just as he imagined, it even crossed his mind to give up and not say anything. It helped that he had already overcome this in his imagination. He had learned that it was okay to think of giving up, but having the thought didn't mean that he had to act on it. Tom's heart was racing and he felt flushed, but he chose his moment and went ahead and spoke up. Actually, once he got started, he quit paying attention to his racing heart and spoke a few sentences. Someone was very interested in what he said and asked him a follow-up question. Even though this was something he hadn't planned for, Tom was able to answer. Needless to say, he left the meeting when it ended with a feeling of pride and accomplishment.

Step 3: Increasing the Risk of Disapproval in Imagination

Tom has already traveled a great distance towards overcoming his phobia. However, there are still things he needs to do to fully recover. Remember that social phobia is at heart a fear of disapproval. To really deal with his phobia, Tom needs to put himself at greater risk for receiving the disapproval he fears.

Tom has learned so far that he is not as likely to make a mistake as he once believed. However, he still fears that if he did make a mistake, it would lead to disapproval from others. Even minor mistakes can be highly disturbing to people with social phobias, who are often "perfectionists." What if Tom continued to talk during meetings, but felt as if he could only say things he had rehearsed so that he would say them "perfectly"? Although that situation might be an improvement over never saying a word, it would not be very comfortable for Tom, and he would still not have overcome his phobia. Tom needs to learn that mistakes usually won't lead to the disapproval he fears, and that, when they do, he can handle it.

Thus, these next two sections involve the practice of making mistakes on purpose—in your imagination at first, and later in real life. They don't have to be big mistakes. In fact, you will want to start out with the smallest mistake you can think of and work your way up to bigger ones. It's good to try and pick a mistake that you are actually worried about making, something relevant to the situation you're working on from your exposure hierarchy. However, for many people with generalized social fears, any kind of mistake practice can be useful. A list of common social "mistakes" can be found below. You may need to use your creativity to come up with mistakes that are particularly threatening to you!

Tom decided that a good mistake related to talking in department meetings would be to lose his train of thought in front of others. This was, in fact, one of his fears—that he would be so overcome with anxiety that he would forget what he was saying. Tom practiced this situation in his imagination until he could do so with minimal anxiety. He imagined himself talking during a meeting and suddenly saying, "I'm sorry. I forgot what I was going to say. It'll probably come back to me later." In his imagined scene, someone made a joke about it, but Tom was able to laugh along without undue concern. It took quite a few repetitions of this scene for his body to habituate to his symptoms of anxiety, and for him to feel confident enough to carry out this mistake in a real-life situation.

Intentional Mistake Practice List

1. Trip in front of someone.

2. Pay for something with the incorrect amount of money.

3. Drop something (for example, a fork, a coin, your glasses) in front of others.

4. Order something that isn't on the menu.

5. Greet someone by the wrong name.

6. Ask for directions to a store, department, etc. in which you are located or which is very close by.

7. Have your hand tremble when paying for something.

8. Take more than the number of items allowed to try on in a clothing store.

9. Underestimate the size of your feet to a shoe salesperson.

10. Have some aspect of your clothing appear inappropriate such as label showing, shirt-tail out, mismatched socks, uncoordinated clothes, fly open (if you're really brave!).

11. Ask for an item that is obviously not carried by the store you are in.

12. Ask an obvious customer for information as if he or she worked at the store.

13. Ask for information or directions and then request that the answer be repeated.

14. Ask a question of someone and either stutter or speak with an unusual accent or tone.

15. Ask someone not to smoke, even though you are in a smoking section.

16. Arrive late on purpose for an appointment.

17. Attempt to purchase something without having enough money along, or without having your checkbook or credit card on hand.

18. Purchase something in a department store and present the wrong charge card.

19. Approach and almost enter the door of a restroom for the opposite sex.

20. Hum or sing so loud that others can hear you.

21. Order some item and change your mind at least twice.

22. Greet or say something to someone across the room at a volume that is noticed by the other people there.

23. Enter a door inappropriately (push when you are supposed to pull or vice versa), push on a door that is locked, try to open the hinged side of the door, etc.

24. Buy something that you would normally be embarrassed to purchase.

25. Walk against the flow of traffic, stop suddenly, or in some other way bring attention to yourself by how you are walking through the mall.

26. Have yourself paged on a public address system.

27. Bump into something.

28. Tell a store clerk that you've lost something, and ask if it's been found.

29. Incorrectly identify the sex of a baby or child to its parents.

Step 4: Increasing the Risk of Disapproval in Real Life

Now you're ready to carry out the same "mistake," but this time in real life. Completing this step will allow you to test your beliefs about what really happens if you make a mistake. You may be surprised to find out that making a mistake is not all that you've feared it to be. That's exactly what happened to Tom.

Tom made enough headway with imaginal mistake practice that he was soon ready to practice making the mistake in an actual departmental meeting. The *in vivo* exposure went much as it had in his imagination. He experienced the usual butterflies ahead of the meeting. He had grown to expect them, especially when he was trying out a new kind of exposure for the first time. The feeling in his stomach wasn't as intense as it used to be, though, and that was nice. As before, while waiting to stage his mistake, he experienced an increased rapid heart rate and some sweating. He was beginning to wonder, though, if anyone really noticed. He was also learning that when he acknowledged these symptoms, but didn't focus on them endlessly, they usually diminished.

A time came during the meeting when Tom decided to make his move. He began speaking, then looked a bit flustered, and said, "Excuse me, I seem to have forgotten what I was going to say." Some of the other officers laughed for a few seconds, and good-naturedly teased Tom about whether he had been out late the night before. Although Tom still felt a little anxious afterwards, he was able to see that his "mistake" was not really a big deal. The meeting continued and, in fact, Tom later had the opportunity to finish what he had begun to say earlier. He was surprised that no more was made of the incident.

Step 5: Coping with Disapproval in Imagination

There's another skill you can learn to take you even further toward overcoming your social fears. Perhaps, like Tom, you've learned that mistakes don't occur as frequently, and aren't as likely to result in disapproval as you once thought. However, you're not yet confident that you can cope with disapproval when it does occur. (And, sooner or later, it does.) You should not have to go through life intimidated by the possibility of disapproval. Therefore, these next two sections involve skills that will help you gain confidence that you can cope with criticism and rejection. First, you'll learn to face disapproval from others in your imagination—much in the same manner as the imagined exposure you've already learned.

Now, you may be thinking, "Why would I want to dwell on the very thoughts that have frightened me and kept me from approaching social situations?" You want to focus on these potential catastrophes because almost all individuals with social phobias have these thoughts periodically. Simply avoiding thoughts of disaster gives you no practice in dealing with them. Although these worst-case scenarios rarely, if ever, occur, thoughts of them can be a real source of distress. This kind of imaginal exposure, used properly, can help you learn to follow up such frightening thoughts with coping statements. You can also learn to habituate to these types of thoughts.

Let's see how this step worked with Tom. When carrying out previous steps in the exposure process, Tom met with a generally positive response from his fellow officers, even when he purposefully made a mistake. Aside from a little joking or teasing, no one made a big deal of the fact that he forgot what he was saying mid-sentence. Tom learned that he didn't have to be perfect all the time. However, he still had nagging thoughts about what would happen if he really did meet with disapproval. What if someone actually criticized him? Would he feel destroyed?

Tom still needed to learn that he can handle disapproval. To this end, he constructed a scene in his imagination in which he makes a mistake, only this time someone does criticize him. When Tom forgets what he saying at the meeting, someone says in an irritated voice, "Get it together, Tom. We don't have all day, you know."

Tom used his paced breathing skills and remembered his coping statements (the one he found most useful was, "I don't have to be perfect.") In addition, he tried to consider the other person's point of view to get a more logical grip on the situation. "Maybe the person criticizing me is having a bad day," he thought to himself. Another thought occurred to him: "He's always so rude, but that doesn't mean I have to get down on myself for being human." By rehearsing this scene until he could do so with a minimal amount of anxiety, Tom prepared himself for coping with a real-life situation in which he made a social gaffe.

Step 6: Coping with Disapproval in Real Life

This is the step in which you learn to handle disapproval in the actual situations you have feared. Sometimes this last step is the hardest to carry out. Even though disapproval is inevitable for everyone at some time, it is difficult to arrange for people to react negatively to you when you want them to. However, it is hard to become confident in your ability to cope with disapproval if you have not demonstrated to yourself that you can handle it in real life. Because it is uncertain whether someone will reject or criticize you when you make mistakes, *in vivo* exposure to disapproval is challenging to arrange. You can act in a way that is likely to provoke disapproval, but there are no guarantees. At the very least, you are now prepared to cope with the negative reactions of other people as they occur naturally. Sooner or later, you will have the opportunity to use your new-found coping skills and learn through experience that disapproval is unpleasant but not catastrophic.

This was, indeed, the case for Tom. As he continued to make comments in department meetings, he on occasion met with disagreement, even disapproval. Tom was prepared for this. He was able to use his deep-breathing skills to keep his bodily symptoms of anxiety manageable. He was able to use his coping statements to remind himself that he didn't have to be perfect or please everyone. What was important was to feel free to say what he wanted, and not to have to monitor every thought before he spoke. He was also able to pat himself on the back for a job well done. His receiving occasional disapproval was actually a sign to Tom that he was taking sufficient risks to overcome his phobia.

What Now?

There's a lot of material in this chapter, presenting a lot of challenges. In fact, this is the core of the treatment section of this book. You should feel comfortable taking the time you need to work through each skill systematically. Don't worry if you don't master all the skills at once—these are techniques that you can practice and improve over your lifetime, tools that you can call on whenever you need them.

After you work your way through all of these steps for one of the low-challenge items on your hierarchy, you need to review your goals and reassess your progress. Look at the remaining low-challenge items. If you think, "These don't frighten me anymore! I know I could manage any of these exposures with ease," you're ready to move up to the medium-challenge category, select an item, and repeat the six techniques detailed in this chapter. For example, Tom made such a dent in his fear of disapproval by practicing exposure techniques with the first low-challenge item that he selected from his hierarchy, that saying grace in front of his immediate family began to seem like a piece of cake.

However, be careful not to move up your hierarchy too quickly. If you have any doubt about your ability to complete all of the exposure items on your low-challenge list, go ahead and repeat the six exposure steps with another item. Then, reassess your progress again. There is great variation among people in how much what is learned in one social situation carries over to another situation. Keep repeating the steps with the low-challenge items until you're convinced that you're ready to move up to the next level. It's okay if you need to tackle each and every one of your low-challenge exposure items before moving on. Remember, your social phobia didn't develop overnight, so it's only natural that it will take time for you to fully overcome your fears. You should move up to the medium-challenge list only when you feel completely sure that you can handle all the items on your low-challenge list. Then repeat the process with your medium-challenge situations until you feel ready to handle the high-challenge ones.

These steps are by no means carved in stone. You can and should tailor this approach to your own particular situation, and your own particular needs. However, if you find that you're confused about how to proceed, or your situation is especially complicated, it may be that you need the assistance of a trained therapist. Chapter 17 will assist you further in knowing when it may be helpful to contact a therapist and what to look for in a mental health professional.

Summary

There is a logical progression of skills to learn in carrying out both imaginal and real-life exposures. The first technique involves entering your feared social situation in imagination; the second skill teaches you how to enter the situation in real life. The third technique gives you the opportunity to experience disapproval in the context of an imaginal exposure. In the fourth technique you hazard that disapproval in real life. The fifth technique describes ways to cope with disapproval in your imagination; and, finally, the sixth skill shows you how to cope with actual disapproval. In the next chapter we'll discuss some basic principles of successful exposure.

10

Principles of Successful
Exposure

When planned and carried out properly, exposures are confidence-build-
ing experiences. You may feel anxious before and during exposure, of
course; but you should have a positive sense of accomplishment when
an exposure is completed. To gain the maximum benefit from your exposure sessions, there are several principles or guidelines you should
keep in mind. These guidelines apply to both imaginal and *in vivo* exposures. If you follow these guidelines, the hard work of exposure is almost certain to pay off!

Go at Your Own Pace

The first important principle of exposure has to do with how to start off,
and how quickly to proceed. Probably the most common way in which
people unintentionally sabotage their recovery is by diving in too fast.
Imagine if you first tried to give a lecture to a group of 100 colleagues
before having practiced making a single comment in a meeting. Would
this be a good idea? Common sense, and research, tell us no. In 1981,
Drs. Andrew Matthews, Matthew Gelder, and Derek Johnson surveyed
the studies done on exposure, and specified the principles of effective
exposure treatment. In most cases, gradual practice was clearly superior
to taking on the most frightening tasks early on.

So, start with the most manageable situations when you begin facing
your fears. You want to be challenged, not overwhelmed. You constructed
a hierarchy, ranking situations from the easiest to the most difficult. Now,
start with an easy item from your low-challenge list. In this way, anxiety
levels remain tolerable. People differ in how long it takes them to gain

this confidence, and to habituate. There is no rigid rule as to when you have mastered a situation, but here are a couple of guidelines.

First, you should have a sense that you could repeat the exposure without major difficulty. If you feel instead that you just barely survived, it's not yet time to move on. If you've mastered an exposure, your anxiety level should not exceed minimal levels. If your level continues to climb, you probably need more practice. You don't have to be perfectly relaxed to say you've mastered an exposure, but you should be relatively comfortable.

Let's look at how one person with a social phobia started out. Ernest, a salesperson at a hardware store, was a very anxious man who felt uncomfortable with neighbors, co-workers—in fact, just about everyone, except two childhood friends. Inviting a group to his home for a party, or asking someone out for a date, were items at the very top of his hierarchy. Taking such steps without laying the groundwork and building up his confidence would have been overwhelming. Most likely, such exposures would have been negative experiences, leaving Ernest more fearful than ever. Instead of starting near the top, Ernest began with the following situation from the list of low-challenge items on his hierarchy: *Greet a neighbor—someone friendly like old Mrs. Jones.*

Ernest found that this exposure, when carried out imaginally, initially raised his anxiety level to a 3 or 4 (based on the "Scale for Rating Intensity of Anxiety" in Chapter 5). As he progressed through the six techniques described in Chapter 9, Ernest's anxiety level rose even higher. But because he had started with a relatively easy situation, his anxiety level remained tolerable. Remember—exposures should bring on moderate anxiety, not panic. On the other hand, exposures should be somewhat challenging—otherwise, no new learning can take place.

The more typical pitfall for people is overambition. An exposure that brings on terror might sensitize you—that is, build an even stronger association in your mind between facing that fear and extreme, unmanageable panic. Of course, even well-planned exposures may bring on a bit more or less anxiety than you expected. If you carefully construct your hierarchy, however, you're likely to stay in the ballpark for optimum learning levels.

You might wonder how you can practice the high-challenge items from your hierarchy, if you need to keep your anxiety level moderate. Fortunately, what seemed like a high-challenge exposure when you first constructed your hierarchy may seem much more moderate after you've experienced some success with lower-level items. When Ernest first began considering exposures, the goal of asking a co-worker to join him for a beer after work seemed as unattainable as climbing Mount Everest. After skills training, and plenty of positive experiences with lower-challenge items on his hierarchy, Ernest began to feel confident that he could attempt this task. Sure enough, he issued the invitation and spent a fairly pleasant hour with a fellow salesman, chatting and watching a ballgame at the local bar. His anxiety level peaked at 6, but diminished quickly.

If Ernest had tried this too soon, he probably would not have managed his anxiety so well. Graduated practice builds a solid foundation for the most difficult exposure challenges. If you find exposures overwhelming, it probably means that you need more practice with easier tasks. After you've built up your confidence you can return to the more challenging situations for another try.

Even if you start out with a challenge that proves to be too difficult for your present level of confidence, it's important to remember that feeling overwhelmed during an exposure is not the end of the world. Occasionally, this can even have the positive effect of showing you that you can survive a very frightening interaction. More commonly, it simply presents a slight setback that can be overcome by more practice with less challenging situations.

Wait until Your Anxiety Level Drops before Ending an Exposure Session

Okay—you've figured out which exposures make sense for starters. What else do you need to keep in mind to get the maximum benefit from facing your fears? A second principle we've found helpful has to do with the length, or duration, of each exposure. Again, the research reviewed by Dr. Matthews and his colleagues offers some guidance: it's best to try to stay in the fear-producing situation until your level of anxiety starts to drop.

If you run away while your fear is still at peak level or climbing, you don't experience the inevitable reduction of symptoms that will occur in any tough situation, given enough time. As a result, you end the session feeling overwhelmed, with little confidence that you could handle a similar situation the next time. You're deprived of the ego boost that comes from staying with an exposure through the worst, and finding out that it's not as bad as you thought. When you wait until your anxiety level drops before leaving an imaginal or *in vivo* exposure session, you can say to yourself, "Hey, I got through this! Anxiety is uncomfortable, but it does pass. I can function in spite of my symptoms. I don't let my fears control me anymore!" Stick it out and you'll gain a sense of mastery.

To illustrate, consider the case of Dorothy, a musician with severe performance anxiety. Planning to play a piece at a piano concert, she makes the necessary preparations. Her anticipatory anxiety is high, and her anxiety level shoots to a 7 just before and during the first few minutes of her performance. If she were to give in to the discomfort and flee the stage before she completes the piece, how would she feel? Like a fool and a failure. She would become so sensitized to the situation that it might take her years to get up the courage to perform again. However, she can go away feeling like a success. Most importantly, she would learn that she can function even when anxious.

Or take the case of Patrick, who had a number of friends but felt anxious at large parties. Naturally, he felt pretty scared at the prospect of walking through the door and greeting people, or getting involved in conversations. He'd panic and think, "Should I turn around and leave?" For Patrick, it was important to wait until he had accomplished a reasonable interim goal (such as talking to three people and staying for half an hour). He can boost his confidence for the next time if he puts off leaving until his anxiety subsides a bit.

Notice that there's no set amount of time you need to remain in an exposure setting. There are several reasons for this. First, people differ. One person's anxiety level may peak in the first minute of an exposure and rapidly decrease thereafter. For another, anxiety may remain quite high for 15 to 20 minutes before it drops off. Again, the rule is to wait until your level drops, if at all possible, before you end the exposure.

Given the nature of social interactions, this may not always be feasible. If you make a phone call that's scary, the person on the other end of the line may say goodbye while your level is at its highest. That's okay. You can still get plenty of benefit from such brief exposures. When you practice such brief exposures, however, you will probably have to repeat them more often than you would need to with longer sessions. Just do what you can to follow the guidelines in most situations. If you're phobic about using public restrooms, try to remain in the restroom until your anxiety level lowers. Don't leave while it's climbing or peaking, if you can help it. This principle applies even with a beginning exposure, which for the bathroom phobic might mean simply entering the washroom, and washing your hands, then leaving. Use your anxiety management skills to bring your level down before you leave.

Practice as Often and as Long as You Can

Let's consider a related principle—how often should you work on exposures? There's an easy answer that takes the form of another question—how quickly do you want to see results? Each person reading this book has a different set of priorities, circumstances, and time commitments. Further, some exposures can easily be carried out without much planning, while the opportunity to do others (such as give speeches) may occur less frequently. Ideally, you should do planned exposures every day; however, this is not always possible. For some people, one or two exposures a week may entail considerable effort. You must decide on a reasonable goal and then work toward it. Obviously, the more often you practice facing your fears, the sooner you'll overcome them.

If you allow too much time to elapse between exposures, you can sabotage your progress. Motivation and confidence have a way of dissolving when days or weeks go by without confronting your anxieties. Fears grow without the feedback that each successful exposure provides—that is, catastrophes are not the usual result of social interactions, and that you can cope with anxiety. In our experience, those who practice exposures frequently develop a strong momentum that helps carry them through the tough times. Conversely, those who procrastinate and delay simply prolong their suffering—they feel guilty, and they extend the unpleasant feeling of anticipatory anxiety. It takes them twice as long to get where they want to be.

Minimize Distractions during Sessions

A fourth principle of successful exposure has to do with minimizing distractions, which can render exposures less effective. By distractions, we mean the way in which some socially anxious people go through the motions of doing an exposure, but somehow remain uninvolved. This is actually a type of avoidance, as we explained in Chapter 1. Research carried out by Drs. P. de Silva and S. Rachman in 1981 confirms that distraction can impede the usual benefits associated with exposure. Let's look at an example of this type of problem.

Beth, who was phobic about eating in front of others, began exposures but reported gaining little confidence, even though she completed each session as planned. A close analysis of her approach to exposures revealed that she was distracting herself from her fears and symptoms every time she ate in the public eye. Rather than recognizing and acknowledging what she felt in these situations, Beth deliberately focused her attention on music being played in the background, the clothing of someone across the room, or thoughts about the decor of the restaurant where she was eating.

At first glance, this might seem like a reasonable coping technique; however, research and clinical experience suggest otherwise. Through these distractions, Beth prevented herself from experiencing significant symptoms. Sounds good, right? Wrong. If you don't experience the symptoms, you can't learn to cope with them. Moreover, distraction is an unreliable ally. It may work on some days but not on others. It never works consistently. Thus, there always comes a day when scary thoughts and feelings strike full force; and when this happens, Beth and others like her are unprepared.

To be truly effective, exposures must provide the opportunity for complete use of all the coping skills you've learned. Practice of these skills is essential to achieving and maintaining a new sense of confidence.

Remember what was said early on in this book: The goal is to learn to manage, not eliminate, anxiety; and this takes practice.

To summarize, distraction, though understandably tempting, is just another form of avoidance. Don't pretend that your heart rate is normal when it's approaching 140 beats per minute. Instead, recognize, accept, and manage your symptoms. Your coping statements might be, "Yes, my heart is racing, but that doesn't mean that anything bad is going to happen. If I relax my body and breathe slowly and deeply, my heart will slow down soon enough. I can do what I need to do in spite of my symptoms."

Evaluate Your Progress Constructively

Are your exposures leaving you with an overall positive feeling? Does it seem that you're making progress toward overcoming your social anxiety? If not, it may be that you are evaluating your exposures in a way that leaves you feeling needlessly discouraged. You could be falling into a common pattern of expecting too much too soon, putting yourself down, not giving yourself credit for what you've accomplished, or using some other maladaptive way of thinking.

These kinds of cognitive errors prevented Rita from recognizing her accomplishments. Rita had taken on several challenging exposures. She completed each, but afterward felt renewed anxiety and distress as she thought over what had taken place. She critiqued her "performance" in such a way that her real achievements seemed tarnished. For example, she mentally reviewed her performance at a political group meeting she regularly attended. Rather than sitting silently as others discussed fund-raising plans, Rita carried out an exposure of giving her opinion as to where the gala fundraiser should be held. She did what she had set out to do, yet she had no sense of accomplishment. Why? Because Rita applied perfectionistic standards to what she had done.

Her suggestion had been the "wrong" one (another location was eventually chosen), and she felt as if her voice had been too quiet and hesitant when she spoke. Rita might have felt justifiably pleased with herself for risking a new behavior, but she persisted in making cognitive distortions that prevented her from realistically evaluating her progress.

Rita needed to review the principles of cognitive restructuring outlined in Chapter 6 to correct her faulty thinking. Once she recognized the distortions, she could talk back to her thoughts as follows:

> *Discouraging Thought:*   The place I suggested for the
>   fundraiser wasn't a good one.
>
> *Healthy Response:*   What's the evidence for that con-
>   clusion? None, really. My opinion is as

valid as anyone else's. I suggested a place that I, and others too, have enjoyed in the past.

Discouraging Thought: My voice was so quiet and hesitant. The other people must have thought I sounded silly and nervous.

Healthy Response: I'm just starting out the work on exposures. Just getting the words out when I'm so anxious is a real accomplishment. Perhaps with more practice I'll sound louder and more assertive, but for now I feel good just for saying what was on my mind. Anyway, it's not helpful to conclude that the rest of the group thought I sounded silly and nervous. That's mind-reading. Most likely they all had different reactions, but most probably had more on their minds than judging me!

Can you speculate on any other cognitive errors Rita may have made? Probability and severity errors in thinking, discussed in Chapters 2 and 6, can also crop up during the evaluation process. Let's look back at Rita's thought, "They must have thought I sounded silly and nervous." Tapping into further associated thoughts, Rita realized that she had followed this up with, "Now others in the group won't want to socialize with me because I'm a loser. I'll never make any new friends in this group."

Do you see some probability and severity exaggerations operating here? How likely is it that others thought she was silly? Even if her estimate about this was accurate (and most likely she overestimated the probability), would this really result in the severe consequence that no one in the group would be interested in her friendship? Rita needs to review her cognitive coping skills. If this applies to you as well, it will be worthwhile to go back to Chapter 6 and review what's written there.

Rita's "failures" were mostly in her head. No real problems had arisen during her exposures. Her overly harsh and critical manner of evaluating what she did was the true difficulty.

At times, however, more concrete problems and disappointments do occur during the exposure process, even though most exposures proceed more smoothly than socially anxious people expect them to. When an exposure leads to a true disappointment, cognitive skills can be especially useful.

Take the case of Ernest, the shy fellow from the hardware store we talked about earlier. After working on general socializing in low-challenge situations, Ernest was ready to ask someone out for a date. In his 36 years, he had never done such a thing! Much anxiety and anticipation preceded this big step. We would love to tell you that the woman Ernest asked out responded enthusiastically, and that they fell in love and got married. Alas, this was not the case. She turned him down. Now the crucial point. Was Ernest devastated? No. He was very disappointed by the experience, but he was not destroyed.

You see, Ernest had prepared himself for this challenging exposure. Part of his preparation entailed imagining what it would be like if the woman said no. Her imagined refusal gave rise to many distressing thoughts; but by using his cognitive coping skills, Ernest was able to put the experience in perspective, even while it was still hypothetical. Below are some of the distorted thoughts he had and the healthy responses he devised with his therapist's guidance.

Discouraging Thought:	What was the point of taking a risk like this? Now I know it's true: women don't find me appealing. I'll always be lonely.
Healthy Response:	I'll never overcome my fears if I don't take risks. Avoiding is what has left me lonely. I know if I persist in asking women out, someone nice and attractive will say yes. One woman's rejection certainly does not mean that all women will turn me down.
Discouraging Thought:	I'll never ask anyone out again. At least that way I don't have to feel like shit when I get turned down. Maybe if I was good looking or made more money, I could get dates; but who wants to date a short, stocky guy with a dead-end job at a hardware store?
Healthy Response:	It hurts to be turned down, but rejection is part of everyone's dating experience. Even the most handsome, richest guys around have been told no. I feel good about the effort I made—it took real courage. If I keep trying, it's sure to pay off; but if I give up, I stay lonely and miserable.

Notice how Ernest reminds himself of two very important things. First, everyone must learn to cope with rejection, even the likes of Julia Roberts or Ted Danson. Realistically, we must all accept that not everyone will respond positively to us in every situation. Such is life. The second crucial thing Ernest remembered was to praise himself. This detail is often neglected, but it shouldn't be. Exposures are hard work, and it's essential to pat oneself on the back for tackling a tough challenge.

Why is it so crucial to evaluate your progress constructively? If you don't, your enthusiasm and confidence for future exposures will wane, and this will only slow your progress down. Above all, each exposure should be a learning experience for you. There are no failures, only opportunities to learn. Whether a session succeeded beyond all imagining, or it was the hardest thing you've ever done, there's something there for you to learn. These lessons can be gathered only one way—through experience!

Keep Reevaluating Your Goals

One final principle of successful exposure remains. It has to do with feeling that you're done. When have you conquered your social phobia? When can you rest on your laurels? This depends to some extent on how impaired you were by your fears, and the level of your goals. If you were only minimally disabled, you'll soon reach a point where you've attained the confidence to lead a normal social life. If you can pretty much do as you like, without unpleasant levels of anxiety, all that remains are some basic maintenance exposures, which are discussed in Chapter 15.

You may, on the other hand, still experience fears that are extensive and crippling. These can require months or years of exposures to overcome, because of the extent of your avoidance, the strength of your maladaptive beliefs, and other factors. Most people can gauge when they are 50, 75, or 90 percent recovered, based on experience and by referring to their original hierarchy. Again, your hierarchy and consideration of your personal goals and objectives, helps you judge whether you're done with your exposure work. Some socially anxious people realistically conclude that there are certain things they never need to do in order to live a full life. It's not necessary that every person with a fear of public speaking must comfortably address an audience of thousands: perhaps talking to a classroom of 30 to 40 students is enough. But if there are situations that remain to be mastered if you are to make the most out of your life, by all means don't stop exposure work prematurely.

Continuing to challenge yourself throughout your life may be the most productive approach you can take. If you are just beginning exposures, this may sound discouraging. Take it on faith, though, that after you become involved in the actual work of facing your fears, this guideline will sound both reasonable and manageable. Exposures can be tremendously satisfying and give you the freedom to enjoy situations you've only dreamed of so far.

Summary

When practicing exposures, it's best to follow several important principles. First, start slowly and gradually work towards facing your most feared social situations. Second, when carrying out an exposure, try to wait for your anxiety level to drop before leaving the fear-producing situation. Third, the more exposures you practice, the more quickly you will overcome your fears. Fourth, minimize distractions during your exposure sessions so that you fully experience the situation. Fifth, reevaluate your goals often, and consider making some form of social exposure a part of your routine for life.

SECTION V

Other Things To Consider

This section was written primarily to address problems that some but not all readers will encounter. If you feel unsure about what to say or do in social situations, you'll be helped by the social skills discussed in Chapter 11. Chapter 12 offers stress management techniques for those who need them, and Chapter 13 examines depression, alcohol abuse, and other problems that often occur in conjunction with social phobia. Chapter 14 gives suggestions for increasing your incentive to recover, while Chapter 15 outlines steps to prevent relapses, and to remedy them if they occur. In Chapter 16, we examine the issue of taking medication for social anxiety, and Chapter 17 tells readers how to find a therapist if one is needed. Chapter 18 points to some future directions for research.

11

What If I Need Other Skills?

Often, people with social phobias are much too hard on themselves. They feel that their social performance is much worse than it actually is, because they have set unrealistically high standards. These people's social skills are okay; it's their self-confidence that's too low. In other cases, social phobias are based, at least in part, on an accurate assessment of one's skills. In other words, some people are afraid of a situation because they realize that their performance in it really will be poor. There is some basic social skill lacking. We call this a social skills deficit. The purpose of this chapter is to help you identify and correct any social skills deficits you may have.

How Are Your Social Skills?

It may be difficult to be objective in answering this question. Individuals with social phobia tend to be overly self-critical and perfectionistic, and are apt to quickly answer, "Terrible. My social skills are nonexistent!" Take your time before jumping to this conclusion. Maybe the best way to realistically assess your social skills is to reflect on any feedback you've gotten from others, or any other type of objective evidence you've received about your social interactions. For example, if you've ever given a speech—maybe in a school or work situation—what has been the response? Did anyone come up to you afterwards and comment that you did a good job? Did you receive an average or above-average grade? If you received some positive feedback, chances are that you're not lacking in skills. Instead, you're judging yourself based upon your self-critical feelings and perceptions, not by how you actually performed.

Let's look at an example of someone who was inaccurately judging herself. Judy had gone all through college without ever having to give a class presentation. When she entered graduate school, she had to take seminars in which presentations were required. For her first several presentations, Judy became extremely anxious, to the point where her stomach was in agony beforehand, and she felt as if everyone could see her chest heaving from breathing so hard. But she received good grades, and her fellow students, when queried, commented that they could not even tell she was nervous. Although Judy felt like a bundle of nerves on the inside, this was not obvious to others, and it didn't hamper her ability to speak effectively. After receiving consistently positive feedback, Judy was able to relax a bit and view her anxiety as a source of energy, rather than a terrible foe that would lead to sure embarrassment. (We'll talk more about public speaking later in this chapter.)

If you've had experiences similar to Judy's in any situation involving social skills, you may not have the deficits you've imagined. Let's consider another brief example. George always felt that he was noticeably quieter than other people. He did not think of himself as outgoing, or even friendly. And yet, much to his surprise, one day at work a fellow employee told George that he really liked working with him. He commented that his conversations with George made the day more pleasant and the time pass more quickly. This unexpected compliment made George stand up and take notice of himself. Maybe he wasn't the most talkative person in the world, but he certainly wasn't the quietest, either. In fact, he was probably just about average.

You may have read the examples above and thought to yourself, "This isn't me. I really do have social skills deficits." Perhaps when you've attempted to give a speech, you didn't receive a good grade or any positive feedback. Maybe you froze or faltered. Or maybe you just don't know how to introduce yourself to a stranger, or how to start a conversation. You have proof! When you go to a party, you're usually the one standing by yourself in the corner, completely unsure about how to approach people. If this is the case, take heart—there's lots of useful material for you in this chapter.

If you're having a difficult time deciding whether you have a social skills deficit, consider the following questions:

- Do you have trouble initiating conversations? Do you wonder what to talk about?

- What about keeping a conversation going? Do your conversations tend to die quickly?

- Do you have a difficult time maintaining eye-contact? Do you smile infrequently?

- What about body language? Do you sit with your arms crossed and your head down?

- Do you tend to say "yes" and "uh-huh" a lot, trying to keep other people talking so that you won't have to?

- Are you reluctant to reveal personal information about yourself?

- Do you tend to stand far away from someone when conversing?

- Do you avoid stating your opinions, or asking for what you want?

- Do you feel unsure about how to make a presentation?

If you answered no to all of these questions, you may not need to spend time refining your skills. However, if you answered yes to even one of the questions, this chapter will likely be of use to you. First we're going to present you with a general game plan for approaching whatever skill you want to master. Then we'll go over a number of particular social skills, such as making a request or giving a speech, and give you tools you can use to improve your skills in this area.

A General Game Plan for Improving Your Social Skills

Okay. You've decided that you want to improve a social skill. Now you need a game plan. Basically, there are four steps to improving your social skills. We'll go over each step briefly here. Then, when we address each of the specific social skills, you'll get a better idea about how this strategy can be applied.

Step 1: Identify the skill deficit. What is it that's missing? For example, maybe you are rather "flat" and expressionless in conversation, leaving others wondering if you're really interested in them or what they have to say.

Step 2: Determine the appropriate social skill to replace the deficit. Step 2 goes hand-in-hand with Step 1. Using the above example, what's missing is a sense of natural animation or appropriate body language. The particular skill to be learned falls under the general heading of nonverbal communication.

Step 3: Experiment with and practice the skill. This step involves experimenting with new behaviors, or practicing new social skills. Staying with the same example, experimenting with nonverbal communication skills might involve practicing in front of a mirror or, if possible, having yourself videotaped. See how it feels to smile more, to use your hands to gesture. If the social skill you need to practice is verbal, use a tape recorder and tape yourself giving a speech or starting a conversation. Go ahead—this is just an experiment! You might feel a little silly at first, but stay with it. Have a little fun.

Step 4: Apply the skill. After you've gained a little confidence experimenting with your new social skill, and you have an idea about what techniques will work for you, apply the skill in a real-life situation. For example, smile and nod your head at a passerby. You might be surprised. You might even get a smile in return.

Now that you have a general game plan in mind, let's discuss particular kinds of social skills in detail.

Nonverbal Social Skills

Much of what we communicate to others is done without ever saying a word. Nonverbal communication skills are basic to good social interactions, serving as the foundation for other, more complex social skills. Most of us learned these skills naturally as we grew up, by watching and "modeling" those around us, and through trial and error. However, for some individuals with social phobias, learning may have been blocked in some way. Although it may have been easier to learn these things as a child, it's never too late. In this section we'll discuss important nonverbal social skills, while the next section covers verbal skills.

Grooming and Hygiene

Despite the old adage, "Don't judge a book by its cover," physical appearance is one of the first things you notice about other people. Although it may seem shallow and superficial, outward demeanor is a short-hand way of gaining initial information about another person. You learn the other person's gender, if it's not otherwise obvious, and may get an idea about a person's age and social standing. Dress and grooming also suggest whether or not an individual seems to care about him or herself. For example, imagine a male co-worker going to work unbathed with his hair uncombed and his shoes torn, wearing the same old grungy, stained sweater day in and day out. You might well wonder if he has any respect for himself, much less for those around him. In most urban contexts, it's just common courtesy to make sure that you're adequately washed and groomed. Of course, it's true that we live in a society that overemphasizes physical attractiveness; and we certainly don't mean to imply that you should try to look like a model. Rather, simply be aware of what type of image you're projecting. Does it match the one you would like to project? Try to find a comfortable style. It doesn't matter if it's simple or snazzy, as long as it feels right to you.

Personal Space

Personal space refers to the area immediately around your body. You've probably had the disconcerting experience of having someone violate your personal space. Perhaps, on a bus, someone has sat down right beside you, despite there having been an empty seat just ahead. Or perhaps you've been bumped by someone's cart while shopping at the supermarket. Personal space research conducted in the 1960's by Dr. E. Hall described four typical distance ranges. *Intimate* distance usually ranges from zero to one-and-a-half feet, and is typically reserved for private interpersonal interactions. *Personal* distance ranges from one-and-a-half to four feet, and is usually used with friends. *Social* distance ranges from four to twelve feet, and is typically used when talking with business or other impersonal acquaintances. Finally, *public* distance is greater than twelve feet and is reserved for such interactions as that between an audience and a performer or speaker. Granted these are just norms, or guides, that vary between different cultures (you certainly won't want to carry a ruler around with you!). Take a look, though, at how you distance yourself around others. Generally, people with social phobias are more likely to stand too far away from their conversational partners; and too much distance may signal to other people that you're not interested in them.

Eye Contact and Other Facial Expressions

You've probably heard the expression, "Eyes are the windows to the soul." Eyes do tell you a lot about another person. Have you ever tried to have a conversation with someone wearing dark glasses? This is such an unnerving experience because it deprives you of eye contact. Eye contact can provide signals about someone's likes and dislikes and immediate reactions. In general, frequent eye contact is a sign of approval, interest, or affection. When you gaze at another person, you're in effect saying, "You interest me." Of course, context is important. Eye contact in which the other person is wide-eyed and smiling is very different from eye contact in which someone is squinting and grimacing at you! Although frequent eye contact is usually a positive experience, one exception exists. Staring—prolonged and intense eye contact—is viewed in most cultures as a threatening nonverbal behavior, and may cause others to recoil in fear. Again, people with social phobias are more likely to err on the side of too little eye contact, not too much.

Other facial expressions are important, too. Some interesting research conducted by Dr. John T. Lanzetta and his colleagues in 1976 and Dr. Miron Zuckerman and his colleagues in 1981 has shown an interesting two-way relationship between facial expressions and our internal emotional states. Not surprisingly, people "show what they feel" by the expression on their faces. For example, smiling usually indicates a feeling of happiness. Crying most often indicates sadness. More interesting, the research revealed that people also "feel what they show." In Dr. Zuckerman's experiment, male and female subjects were divided into three groups and shown videotapes of either pleasant, neutral, or negative scenes. Then each of these groups was further divided and given separate instructions. One-third of each group was told to suppress their facial expressions, one-third was told to exaggerate them, while the other third group was not given any instructions about facial expressions. While watching the videotapes, the subjects' physiological responses were monitored; after viewing the tapes, they were also asked to rate their emotional responses. Can you guess the results? Subjects who had exaggerated their facial expressions were both more physically reactive and rated their emotional experiences more intensely than the subjects who had suppressed their facial expressions.

So what does this have to do with social skills? It means that if you learn to appear more relaxed and comfortable in a social situation, there's a good chance that you may learn to feel more relaxed and comfortable as well.

Too often, people with social phobias fail to show a variety of facial expressions, almost as if their faces were immobilized with fear. It's important to go ahead and try to move those facial muscles anyway—let a big smile ease gently over your face, for example. See if you don't notice a change in the way you feel! One other reminder, though. Try to notice whether your facial expressions, are in fact appropriate to your feelings. It's common for people with social phobias, who don't want to ruffle other's feathers, to smile when they actually feel something entirely different—such as anger. Have you ever noticed someone else laughing while describing a very painful experience or emotion? Laughter can be a way of denying or discounting other, negative feelings. For people to take you seriously, it's important that your nonverbal behaviors are congruent with the message you want to deliver. We'll talk more about this issue when we discuss assertiveness in the next section.

Body Posture and Gestures

The way you position your body in relation to the person with whom you're talking is another subtle cue about your feelings. If you have your arms crossed and are leaning away from the other person, you may be communicating disinterest, hostility, or fear. In contrast, if you're leaning slightly forward, have your arms in a relaxed position, and are facing your conversation partner, your mood will more likely be interpreted as friendly and involved. Try to hold your head up high. Too many people with social phobias tend to keep their gaze on the floor, as if looking for a contact lens! Also watch what you do with your arms and hands. When you're nervous, it's not uncommon to fidget with something in your hands, perhaps a pen or a paper clip. This is a tip-off to others that you're uncomfortable, and can lead them to feel edgy as well. Practice letting your arms rest gently on your lap, or on the sides of the chair; but don't be so stiff that you can't use your hands and arms to help you describe something, or to add emphasis. It can help to do an abbreviated version of your paced breathing and relaxation exercises before and even during a conversation.

There's a lot to concentrate on and remember here, but with practice these skills will become second nature.

Verbal Social Skills

In this section we'll go over a variety of verbal social skills, the basics of what you need to know. If this proves to be insufficient for your particular needs, a list of additional readings is included at the end of the chapter.

Making Telephone Calls

Making telephone calls can be a frightening experience for people with social phobias, particularly for people with generalized phobias. One woman seen at our clinic felt unable to initiate any telephone calls, and rarely answered the phone when she was home alone. The difficulty seems to lie in the unpredictable nature of telephone calls—you never know what the person on the other end of the line will be like, friendly and helpful, or curt and gruff. Although you can't control the other person's words or mood, using proper telephone etiquette may stack the odds in favor of receiving a positive response or making a good impression.

First of all, prepare yourself, even before dialing. If you're making a business call, jot down a few notes about the important points you want to cover. If it's a personal call, you may not need this step (although it can't hurt). When you place the call, allow the telephone to ring ten times. That will give the person approximately one minute to answer the call. There's nothing more annoying than rushing inside to answer the phone, only to have the caller hang up after four or five rings. When someone answers, simply state, "Hello, this is John Doe. Is Mary Smith there?" If you intend to take more than a minute or two of the person's time, it's polite to ask whether this is a convenient time for the call, or if it would be better to call back later. If you only need a minute, tell the person at the outset, and then stick to your plan. When ending a business call, be sure and thank the person for his or her time. When ending a personal call, you may need only say something to the effect of, "I enjoyed talking with you," or "I'll talk to you again soon."

You can include practice with placing and receiving phone calls as part of your exposure sessions. Remember, you can begin with imaginal exposure and work your way up to *in vivo*. Be creative in staging your exposure sessions. Perhaps you could use two extensions on your home phone and practice making phone calls with a nonthreatening friend or family member. You might also set up times when such a person would actually call you, to gain practice in answering the phone. Begin with having the person call at a specified time (to give you the comfort of an element of predictability). As you progress, have the person call at an unspecified time, or within a range of a few hours when you plan to be home. Also remember to use your paced breathing and cognitive coping skills to manage your anxiety before, during, and after the exposure. The section that follows on conversational skills will also aid you in mastering the telephone.

The Art of Conversation

Some people have an aversion to learning conversational skills, mistakenly thinking that the function of small talk is by definition limited to generating meaningless and idle chatter. Small talk actually serves a number of important functions. First of all, it shows respect for other people and their psychological boundaries. Rather than diving right in with intimate and personal questions, it's better to approach someone gradually, following recognized social conventions. Small talk is a sort of diversion that allows you and another person to exchange nonverbal social signals that can help you decide whether to start a more in-depth conversation. Is the other person smiling? Is his or her body language receptive? Is your overture being interpreted in the right spirit? Keep your eyes and ears open to such signals during the small-talk phase of a conversation; and make sure that *your* nonverbal social signals are sending out the message you want to give. These nonverbal messages are part of the art of conversation as well!

You don't need a fancy opening line to start a conversation; you're best off sticking to sincerity and authenticity. Simply saying hello and introducing yourself can be quite sufficient. If you're at a party, a nice addition to giving your name is to tell the other person your relationship to the host or hostess. For example, "Hi! My name is Charlie Goodman. I work with George." You have a natural link to anyone at the party, because everyone there presumably is somehow connected to the host or hostess. A follow-up question after introducing yourself could be, "How do you know George?"

After the introduction phase, you're going to have to assume some responsibility for keeping the conversation going if you want the conversation to continue. Anxiety over what to talk about is often mentioned by people who are nervous about dating. Whether it's a new friend, or a potential new boyfriend or girlfriend, the same principles apply. You should take an active part in moving the conversation along. Too often people with social phobias leave that burden to others. But depending solely on the other person to maintain and nurture the conversation puts you in a vulnerable position. When you refuse to be responsible, you also surrender control of the outcome—and a very charming and delightful person may walk out of your life forever. Keep your goal in mind during the conversation (a date, a business connection, a long-term romance)—and keep those nonverbal messages as clear and earnest and appropriate as what you choose to say with words.

Let's go over several key strategies for keeping a conversation alive and well.

Asking Questions. One of the most important rules is to use open-ended questions. Closed questions are those that can be answered with a simple yes or no, and do nothing to nudge a conversation forward. They put the ball back in your court all too quickly. For example, if you ask someone, "Do you like your job?" the other person could simply reply with, "Yes." After that, you're stuck with thinking of something else to say. Also, a barrage of closed questions can give the other person the uncomfortable feeling of being cross-examined rather than drawn out.

Open-ended questions, on the other hand, require the other person to elaborate, demanding more than a one-word response. They communicate to other people that you're interested in the way they express themselves, and in the subtleties of their thoughts and feelings, in a way closed questions do not. In general, people like to talk about themselves, especially if the other person communicates genuine interest. Next time you listen to a talk-show host, notice how she or he uses open-ended questions to bring the interview to life.

Letting Your Vulnerability Show. Rather than demanding a stranger's opinion or confidences, it's fine to offer your own. In fact, it can be a very effective ice-breaker to simply tell someone, "I'm always so nervous at parties!" or "I never know what to say to someone to break the ice." It's okay to show some vulnerability; it can be much more appealing than the smoothest come-on line. (*Most* people feel nervous, at least to some degree, at parties; and *most* people feel somewhat daunted at the prospect of initiating a social interaction with a stranger, especially an attractive one.) In other words, don't try to put one over on someone else by pretending to be cool, suave, and aggressive—be yourself, and have some faith that an open, caring manner is worth lots and lots of social mileage.

Listening. Another important way to keep things moving is to become a skilled listener. This may not sound too difficult, but it can be harder than you think: listening is not just a passive skill. If you're anxious and caught up in your own worries (Can she tell I'm sweating? My heart is sure racing!), you're liable to show, in your manner or responses, that you're not paying attention. The other person may not know what's going on with you. He or she may simply interpret your inattention as indifference. Remember that other people have their own insecurities, too. They want to be liked, to feel that they're being interesting and entertaining. One useful technique for conveying your interest is to use *active* listening skills. Paraphrase or reiterate what the person has said: "What I hear you saying is…." or "That's so interesting that you think…." (Don't function as an echo, though. You want to build on what the other person has said, rather than just repeat it.) Another slightly more difficult active-listening skill is to reflect back to the person the feeling you heard communicated. For example, if someone is talking about not liking their job, you could say something like, "That sounds like it must be frustrating." If you don't get the feeling exactly right, that's okay. The other person may correct you. "Frustrating isn't the word. I'm so burnt out I can hardly stand it." Even if you're off the mark at first, people will appreciate it that you're trying to understand them.

It can be a useful exercise to spend some time eavesdropping on other people's conversations (cafes are good places for this; so are buses). Are people using active listening skills? Is each person really responding to what the other has said; or are they both just following their own agenda, using the other person as a sounding board? What are they saying with their body language that they're not saying with their words?

You may be surprised at how generally inarticulate most people are in their conversations. The clever dialogue one hears in movies and reads in books has been constructed by artists: real dialogue, when transcribed, often sounds like a lot of gibberish. Especially in America, people tend to speak in half-articulate grunts and incomplete sentences. So be easy on yourself when you don't come across with the clever smoothness of a Raymond Chandler character! If you're really listening, and really responding, you're one-up on most Americans for conversational skills.

Self-Disclosure. Sharing your thoughts and feelings, your impressions and associations, can be a very scary prospect if you have a social phobia. Your natural inclination may be to keep yourself hidden to the greatest extent possible; and, if exposure is necessary, to wear a mask. Perhaps you feel that if people knew the "real" you, they would turn away in revulsion.

Such feelings are a function of poor self-esteem rather than a reflection of reality. You can use the skills you learned earlier about refuting maladaptive thoughts ("I'm a caring and decent person, and I have as much right to make meaningful social connections as anyone else at this party.") If you don't disclose anything about yourself, people may misinterpret your stance as aloof and uncaring, or even contemptuous.

As we noted earlier, when you're first getting to know someone, you'll want to gauge what you disclose about yourself. At a party, talking with someone for the first time, you probably won't want to talk in detail about the bitter, messy divorce you just went through. Rather, keep the conversation light in the beginning. Talk about your interests—a book you've just read, a new movie that's out, or the kind of work you do. It's a good idea to try and keep abreast of current events. That way you'll always have a wealth of conversational topics. Later, when actually developing a relationship or friendship with someone, you can disclose more personal information. Use your judgment, and try to keep your end of the conversation appropriate to the mood and the circumstances. (When the other person leans back and comments on the beauty of the stars, and how stars always make him/her feel passionate and romantic, this is *not* the moment to recap the latest stories from *Newsweek*.) Timing is important. You don't want to share too much too soon—although this is rarely a pitfall for people with social phobias. One way to judge whether you're going at a pace that's comfortable for the other person is to gauge your disclosures to theirs. If you share your feelings about something and this does nothing to threaten the comfort level of the conversation, the other person is likely to share something of about the same intensity. This isn't a hard-and-fast rule, just a guideline. Take your cues from the circumstances, the context, and, most of all, the other person's mood. He or she will let you know if you're on target.

Giving and Receiving Compliments

Giving and receiving compliments is another important social skill. Giving someone a compliment can be a good way to get a conversation going; but there are a few things to keep in mind. First of all, compliments should be genuine! Don't say you like someone's tie if inside you're thinking, "That's the most hideous color I've ever seen." Try to make your compliment specific—it will be more meaningful that way. If you simply say, "You look nice today," or "I like your outfit," the other person doesn't know specifically what you like. Rather, say something such as, "I like the way your scarf matches your dress so well." And remember—compliments don't have to be based only on appearances. In fact, the most meaningful compliments often refer to other aspects of a person's behavior or personality (for example, "You really seem to have a way with children!" or "That was a fabulous presentation").

Receiving compliments can be difficult if you've been raised to be modest and self-effacing. Unless you're in Japan or some other culture where modesty is *de rigueur*, you should resist the impulse to protest when someone gives you a compliment. A compliment is like a gift, and this is like turning your nose up at someone's gift—very ungracious behavior indeed! Protesting or disagreeing can make others feel foolish for complimenting you in the first place. At the very least say, "Thank you" as a way to acknowledge what the other person has said. If possible, try to add something else so that the person knows you appreciate the compliment. For example, you could say, "Thank you. I looked a long time to find a scarf that would match this dress. I'm so pleased you noticed!"

Assertive Communication Skills

As a result of your social anxiety, you may have difficulty expressing some of your thoughts and feelings openly. If this is a problem for you, you need to work on your assertive communication skills. We have seen some people at our clinic who were reluctant to work at becoming more assertive because they thought we were suggesting that they become pushy or obnoxious. Nothing could be further from the truth!

Assertive communication is the direct and honest expression of your thoughts, feelings, and wants, while keeping in mind and respecting the rights and feelings of other people. When you behave assertively, you express yourself in a nonjudgmental, non-threatening manner. You take responsibility for your own actions. The goal of assertiveness is communication.

Passive communication and *aggressive communication* are two alternative but inferior styles for getting your point across.

Passive communication involves an unwillingness to express your thoughts and feelings openly. It's usually a result of such maladaptive thoughts as, "They'll get angry," "They won't like me," "I can't handle conflict, so it's better to avoid it," "I don't have any right to complain." When you communicate passively, you are giving into other people's wants and needs at the expense of your own. You are likewise refusing to take responsibility for your own happiness, hoping instead that someone else will be able to read your mind and respond to your needs. This may be a nice fantasy, but it's a very impractical way to try to get your needs met. The unexpressed goal of passive communication typically is to avoid the anger or disapproval of other people.

Aggressive communication, on the other hand, is characterized by asserting your needs or desires in a manner that disregards the feelings of other people. If you express yourself in this way, you'll come across as pushy, selfish, and unwilling to negotiate. Often the goal of aggressive communication is to inflict hurt (before *you* get hurt) or to get back at someone for a prior wrong. In other cases, someone may simply not have matured enough emotionally to use a more socially acceptable communication style (two-year-olds are typically aggressive in expressing their wants and needs).

Each of the above types of behavior has consequences. If you learn to be assertive, you are more likely to get your needs met, because other people will be aware of what you want without having their feelings trampled on. Some people who are more used to a passive style feel "selfish" when they try to behave more assertively. Keep in mind that assertiveness is generous, in that you're sending people clear signals about what you want, while giving them the opportunity to refuse you if your needs conflict with theirs.

In contrast, when you communicate aggressively, you are likely to have difficulty getting along with other people. You may cause others to feel angry and resentful, and may have even greater difficulty getting what you want. Passive behavior, on the other hand, may lead you to feel anxious, angry, depressed, and helpless. Again, you are not likely to get your needs met if you don't express them; and other people may experience frustration or discomfort when interacting with you if you don't assert your own needs.

You may be thinking, "This makes sense, but how can I actually become more assertive?" Perhaps the most important communication skill you need to practice is expressing yourself with *I*-statements. An *I*-statement is a sentence that begins with the word "I" and communicates directly what you are thinking or feeling. Here are some examples of *I*-statements:

- I'm happy that you asked me to dinner.

- I feel angry that you made fun of me in front of other people.

- I would like to go see a movie this weekend.

- I know you have been stressed out at work, but I need more time with you.

Now that you have a general understanding of what it means to be assertive, let's go over two important assertiveness skills especially useful for people with social phobias: making requests and refusing requests.

Making requests. Making requests can be a difficult task for people with social phobias. You may feel that you don't have the right to ask for something you want. The best way to get around this maladaptive belief is to subject it to logical refutation, as we discussed in earlier chapters ("Don't I have as much right as anyone else to ask for what I want? What is it about me that makes me particularly undeserving of getting my needs met? Would an outside observer agree that this is logical and fair?"). With practice and by changing your maladaptive beliefs, you can learn to ask for what you need. Of course, asking doesn't guarantee that you'll get what you want—but it certainly improves your chances!

For example, let's imagine that you would like your spouse to help clean the house before your parents come over for dinner. An assertive request would be: "I would like the house to look nice when my parents arrive. I'd really appreciate it if you would vacuum the family room." Notice how specific and direct the request is. Your spouse has a clear message as to what would be pleasing to you.

A far less effective approach would be to make an aggressive criticism of your spouse's behavior: "You never help around here and the house is a mess." Your spouse is likely to respond defensively; and might start pointing out how he or she does help around the house. As you can see, this could easily turn into an argument, and is unlikely to get you the desired result.

If you were passive in making your needs known, you might say something like this: "I wish the house looked better for when my parents come over." This may have no effect on your spouse (you haven't given any cues about what he or she might do to help); and you may end up feeling frustrated that your hidden agenda wasn't simply intuited. Lots of passive people—and lots of spouses—fall into the trap of expecting their intimates to be mind-readers. No matter how close the two people are, they still need to communicate their needs with clarity and precision if their relationship is to last over the long haul. People who love you will appreciate it if you tell them how they can contribute to your happiness and well-being.

Let's take another example that may hit close to home for some of you—asking someone for a date. This is a difficult request to make for several reasons. For one thing, it's typical for just about anybody's anxiety to increase in this situation, which is rife with possibilities for rejection. You are putting yourself on the line with someone whose response is very important to you—and that's not easy. To make matters worse, you have no control over whether or not the other person will accept.

There are, in fact, several things you can do to increase the odds of a favorable response. First of all, don't just say: "Are you busy Friday night?" This is one of those closed questions we discussed earlier. It's easy for the other person to say "Yes, I'm busy"—and you still don't know whether he or she would be interested in going out with you.

Instead, you might say something like, "I've been wanting to see the new Spike Lee movie. Have you seen it yet?" Although this is still a closed question, it gives the other person the opportunity to respond (Yes or No), to make an I-statement ("I've been wanting to see it, too" or "I hate Spike Lee movies!"), and to encourage you, if this is what he or she wants to do ("I've been meaning to go, but I didn't want to go by myself—sometimes those crowds are just nuts!"). If the object of your interest seems intrigued, you can then follow through by arranging an exact day and time. Try to be simple and clear; and keep your body language in line with your feelings. If you are a woman, remember that it's perfectly okay for you to ask a man out for a date. Times—thank goodness!—have changed.

Don't feel that asking someone out requires overwhelming presence or charm. Smile, make eye contact, and keep your posture open—these are the important things to remember. A friendly, direct approach works best. Say you've met someone at a party or class whom you'd like to know better. Simply tell him or her how you feel, and follow your *I*-statement with an assertive request. "I've enjoyed our conversation so much. Would you like to have dinner with me this weekend?" Or you might say something like, "I've been thinking it would be fun to get together outside of class. I usually go hiking on Sundays—would you like to join me?"

If the person you'd like to date turns you down, be gracious, and leave the door open to future possibilities. "I'm sorry you can't make it. Let me know if you'd like to get together another time."

It's unproductive—and bad for your self-esteem—to keep going over the circumstances of a rejection. Give yourself a pat on the back for trying, and get on with your life. As the old saying goes, there are other fish in the sea!

Refusing Requests. This is another tough one for people with social phobias. How often have you agreed to do something only to regret it later? Being assertive about what you *don't* want is just as important as being assertive about what you *do* want.

The first step in this process is to assess whether or not a request is reasonable. Only you can decide this. What may be reasonable to one person may be completely out of the question for another. You have to consider your own situation (in other words, you must consider—and respect—your own needs). Your inclination is also an important factor. Maybe you just have a gut feeling that you want to say no. Or perhaps you need more information before you can make a decision. For example, you might ask the other person, "If I agreed, what would it entail?" It's also okay to stall for time and say, "I need to think about it." Once in a while, an immediate response is necessary, but this isn't usually the case. It's much better to take the time to consider carefully than to say yes when you just can't deliver the goods—this will only cause embarrassment later on. If you are feeling hesitant, manipulated, or trapped, this may be a sign that you want to say no. Listen to your feelings. People with social phobias tend to give more importance to other people's needs than to their own, which makes saying no especially hard for them.

How do you refuse a request? As directly as possible. Give a simple no, and skip the long-winded justification. If you feel compelled to give a reason, keep it brief. Try to avoid apologizing excessively. For example, perhaps a friend asks if you'll take care of her kids for two nights while she's out of town on a business trip; but the dates overlap with a one-week visit by your father and his wife. You'll already have a full house and all the guests you can handle. You might say, "I'd really love to; and under other circumstances I'd say yes. But my dad and his wife will be visiting then, so I'll have to say no." You've made your position clear, and have said no without alienating your friend. You've also considered—and respected—your own needs.

Making a Presentation

We've saved this topic for last for two reasons. First, many of you will find this skill to be the most daunting among the ones we've reviewed so far. Second, making a presentation is a complicated task that involves many of the verbal and nonverbal social skills we've already discussed. We'll present you with a general guide here, but again, entire books have been written on this topic. Please refer to the related readings at the end of the chapter if you want to learn more.

Preparing Your Presentation

Before starting to prepare your presentation, you need to ask yourself a couple of important questions. First of all, who is your audience? What are their characteristics? Are they highly educated? Will they be women, men, or a mixture? What is the general range of their ages? Are they there because they want to, or is attending this presentation some sort of requirement? The more you know about your audience, the better you will be able to target your presentation specifically to them. Second of all, what do you want to get across to the audience? Do you want to inform? Entertain? Convince? What's the general thrust or theme of your presentation? The answers to these questions should be clear in your mind before you begin.

Needless to say, you can expect to experience some anxiety anticipating the upcoming presentation. Don't allow your anxiety to take over, however. If you "try not to think about it," and, consequently don't prepare, you'll really have something to worry about on the big day! Depending on the length and nature of your presentation, it's best to give yourself several weeks to prepare.

Take an adequate amount of time to write down your main ideas. What are the major points you want to make? Under each of these important points, list information you'll use to illustrate your points. Maybe you have a descriptive story to back your point, or a telling statistic. These major points and your back-up information will form the main structure of your presentation. How you order them will depend on the nature of your speech (most speeches tell a story of some kind; and every good story requires a beginning, a middle, and an end). Write these points in terms of key words on numbered 3x5 or 5x7 cards—but don't write out each point verbatim. You want to *tell*, not *read*, a story to your audience.

The next step is to prepare your opening statement. The first sentence or two should be something that will grab the audience's attention. This could be an anecdote relevant to your topic, or one that your audience can personally relate to. It could be some type of surprising statistic. Although you can open with a humorous comment, make sure that you're completely comfortable with this approach. There's nothing more dampening to a speaker's spirits than telling a joke that doesn't come across. Don't forget that stand-up comedy is a skill that performers take years to learn.

In contrast to the body of the talk, it's a good idea to write out your opening sentence word for word. Even memorizing it is okay. This will help you feel less anxious. In most situations, it's unnecessary and even detrimental to memorize the rest of your talk. (Exceptions would be cases in which your talk may be extensively quoted and analyzed by the press—in such cases you'd probably want some degree of control over every word that came out of your mouth. Fortunately, few people have to face such situations!) Usually it's best to talk to the audience directly, referring to your key points as needed.

So you've got the opening and the body of your talk prepared. Now all you need is the closing. In many situations, this is the time to tell your audience what kind of action you would like them to take as a result of attending your presentation. If you've presented some controversial information, maybe all you can reasonably ask them to do is to consider the information you've presented with an open mind. Perhaps you'd like them to write their local government representatives about the topic you've discussed. Another presentation may call for some other type of action or simply a reaction if your speech was dramatic or emotional. The concluding statement is the only other part of your speech you may want to write out word for word.

Use simple and direct language in your speech. Presentations are not the time to try and impress people with big words (although, again, the language you use will depend on your audience). When writing out your cards, print or type your key points and opening and closing statements in large letters. Leave plenty of spaces between lines. You might want to use several different colors of ink. The main point is to be able to read your cards with ease when giving your presentation.

Practicing Your Presentation

Try to complete the above steps at least several days before the actual date of your presentation. It would be nice to have a week left at this point; but we understand that in today's busy society, this may not always be possible. Anyway, the more time the better.

The next thing you need to do is to practice and time your presentation. This will help you know if you need to provide more information or cut some out. Running through your talk at least several times will help boost your confidence. You've got a couple of options for structuring your practice sessions.

First of all, with an exposure of this magnitude, it's a good idea to do some imaginal work before progressing to *in vivo* practice. Review the techniques in Chapter 9 for carrying out imaginal and *in vivo* exposure sessions. Remember to include some "mistake practice" as part of your preparation. When you're ready to get some actual practice giving your presentation, enlist the aid of a friend or family member. Give them your presentation. Have them give you feedback. Did you talk too fast, move your hands about nervously? Did you talk loudly and clearly? Did they understand the major points you were trying to make? Was the length appropriate? Make sure you pick someone who will give you constructive feedback. An additional option is to tape your talk on an audio or video cassette and then critique your presentation. Now don't be too hard on yourself. The goal is to learn from this practice session, not to criticize every little thing. You may need to practice your presentation several times—and to do some editing—before you feel comfortable with its contents. If possible, try and practice at least once in the actual place where you'll give your talk.

Giving the Presentation

It's the actual day of the presentation. You've prepared your talk thoroughly. You've practiced. You're ready. But you've got a case of the jitters!

That's okay. Even famous performers like Joan Rivers and Barbara Walters admit to still being nervous before making an appearance. So what do they do? People who routinely perform in front of others have learned how to make their nervousness work for them. In effect, they transform anxiety into excitement. Do what you can to manage your anxiety before and during the talk (see Chapter 5); but whatever nervousness is left over, you'll do best to label as enthusiasm and excitement, rather than fear and anxiety. Think about how much you have to share with your audience. After all, you probably wouldn't have been asked to talk to the group unless you had something valuable to offer. In most cases, your audience will be a supportive one; they're not there to make your life miserable!

You'll probably be introduced by someone before your presentation actually begins. After the introduction, thank the person and then greet your audience. If you have a friend in the audience, make eye contact with him or her right away. That will give you confidence. If you don't know anyone in the audience, pick a friendly face to focus on for a moment. Then take a deep breath and begin. You've got your cards to rely on. Glance at them periodically, but don't read. Remember—you shouldn't have written out your cards word for word, except for possibly your opening and closing comments. Make frequent eye contact with your audience (or the camera, if you're appearing on t.v.) throughout the presentation. Use gestures when appropriate, but try to keep nervous movements (flicking your hair, adjusting your clothes) to a minimum.

After your presentation is complete, you may choose to have a question and answer session. Some people prefer to encourage their audience to ask questions throughout, while others find this distracting and ask their audience to hold their questions to the end. A few pointers on the Q and A phase. If no one asks questions right way, don't panic. It doesn't mean they didn't enjoy your presentation. People in an audience may be a little inhibited at first when they're asked to call attention to themselves as individuals. You can help them out by having a question prepared yourself. You might say, "I'm often asked about _____." This will usually be enough to get people started. When people do ask questions, it's a good idea to repeat the question to make sure that everyone hears it. Make sure that you listen, too! It's all right to pause to consider your answer. And don't be afraid to say, "I don't know," if you don't. Also, be patient with your audience. It's common for someone to ask a "stupid" question or one that you already answered in your talk (or even to repeat someone else's question!) You, of all people, should be understanding about the nervousness that produces audience blunders.

A final tip: don't run over the allotted time. If your presentation was scheduled to last half an hour, keep it to that if at all possible. People may have other places they need to go. It's much better to end on time than to have people fidgeting or leaving in the middle of your question and answer session. As the great impresarios say, "Leave them wanting more!"

After the presentation is over, let yourself feel the much-deserved pride in your accomplishment. It's said that among the population at large, fear of public speaking is rated even above the fear of death! Resist the urge to analyze every detail of your talk, or the audience's reaction in attempts to find fault with your performance. Public speaking is a cumulative skill: the more you do it, the better you'll get.

What If I Need More Help Learning Social Skills?

Learning social skills can be a difficult task for anyone. We've only been able to provide a very brief overview in this chapter, which may not be sufficient for some of you. Keep in mind that other resources are available. We've included some recommended readings below. You also may want to check with your community colleges, which frequently offer continuing education courses on such topics as assertiveness training. There are also groups, such as Toastmasters, which help those wanting to improve their public speaking skills. You may want to consider seeking professional help if you need extra guidance and support (see Chapter 17).

Summary

Sometimes people's social fears can be related to actual ignorance or lack of practice with particular social skills. For example, an individual may not know how to start a conversation or ask someone out for a date. This chapter reviewed the basics of verbal and nonverbal communication skills, and included a brief primer on how to make a presentation.

Recommended Readings

Alberti, R. and M. Emmons (1970) *Your Perfect Right: A Guide to Assertive Behavior.* San Luis Obispo, CA: Impact.

Bloom, L., K. Coburn, and J. Pearlman (1976) *The New Assertive Woman.* New York: Dell.

Desberg, P., and G.D. Marsh (1988) *Controlling Stagefright: Presenting Yourself to Audiences from One to One Thousand.* Oakland, CA: New Harbinger Publications.

Hanigan, M. (1980) *Secrets of Successful Speaking.* New York: Collier Books/ MacMillan Publishing Company.

Hoff, R. (1988) *I Can See You Naked: A Fearless Guide To Making Great Presentations.* New York: Andrews and McMeel: Universal Press Syndicate Company.

12

What If Stress Interferes with My Progress?

By following the methods outlined in this book, you may have made considerable progress toward recovering from your social phobia. Some people, however, find that other life stressors limit their progress. If this is the case for you, this chapter could be an important part of your individualized recovery plan.

Defining Stress

You probably have a general idea about what it means to be "stressed out." But what actually is stress? Stress is the wear and tear on your body that results from the demands of life. We call these demands *stressors*. For example, financial or health difficulties may consume much of your energy and leave you feeling stressed. You may develop nagging headaches or other physical problems. Stress is not just the result of negative events, however. Positive events, such as getting married or beginning a new job, can also lead to stress. We'll help you examine your personal sources of stress in a later section.

You cannot completely eliminate stress from your life; in fact, you wouldn't want to. Everyone needs some stress to feel alive and vital. Imagine if you never had a new challenge to face! You might become awfully bored—which can be stressful in and of itself. While you can't eliminate stress, you can learn how to manage it more effectively. In doing so, you can become healthier, as well as learn to feel more comfortable and more in control.

How Your Body Reacts To Stress

Hans Selye, often called the father of stress research, described three stages of physiological change your body undergoes when under stress. The first of these is called the *alarm stage*. When you initially encounter a stressful situation, your body prepares itself for "fight or flight." During this time your heart rate, perspiration, and breathing all accelerate. Your pupils dilate and your bloodstream is flooded with stored energy. These physiological changes are helpful in the short run, enabling you to meet the demands of the situation. Next, your body moves into the *resistance stage*, during which your immunity to illness increases above the normal level. Finally, however, your body becomes overworked, and you move into the *exhaustion stage*. During this period, your body is depleted of its normal energy reserves and your resistance to illness decreases. The precise timeframe of this process will vary, based upon several variables, including individual differences and the nature and severity of the stressor.

What this means is that if you're under chronic stress, your body may suffer. An explosion of recent research has demonstrated that stress probably plays a factor in hypertension, coronary heart disease, migraine and tension headaches, ulcers, and asthmatic conditions, to name a few. In addition, chronic stress may exacerbate many other medical problems, such as arthritis, allergies, skin diseases, and gastrointestinal disturbances. Even if you don't experience any of these conditions, other symptoms of chronic stress may plague you, such as irritability and fatigue.

Because your body and mind are so closely connected, stress also plays a role in your emotional well-being. If you're under too much stress, you may be more susceptible to anxiety and depression. In fact, you may not have the energy you need to devote to your social phobia recovery plan.

Benefits of Managing Your Stress

In case you're not yet convinced that stress management is a good idea, here's a list of some of the benefits of learning to become more relaxed in your daily life.

- You'll reduce your general level of anxiety.

- You can increase your energy and raise your productivity level.

- You'll fall asleep more easily and sleep more soundly.

- You'll increase your ability to focus and concentrate.

- You'll feel less irritable.

- You'll decrease the chances of developing psychosomatic disorders, such as ulcers, migraine headaches, and so on.

Identifying the Stressors in Your Life

The first step in learning to manage your stress is to assess where it's coming from. In our modern-day world, there are more sources of stress than in any other period of history. The following exercise will help you locate the various sources of stress in your life. Check off any items below that reflect your experience.

Stressors in My Life

☐ **Physical stressors.** *Example:* You work under the pressure of constant deadlines, frequently working late into the night, often sleeping too little and eating fast food on the run.

Note any physical stressors:_____

☐ **Illness or injury stressors.** *Example:* You recently hurt your neck and back in a car accident. Now you have difficulty doing your regular desk job and have to make frequent trips to the chiropractor.

Note any illness/injury stressors: _____

☐ **Family stressors.** *Example:* You are experiencing continuing conflict with a relative. Another example would be taking care of an aging parent.

Note any family stressors: _____

☐ **Work stressors.** *Example:* Feeling unhappy or "burned out" on your job. Other examples include conflict with boss, having too much to do, long commutes, and so on.

Note any work stressors: _____

☐ **Financial stressors.** *Example:* You were recently laid off from work and are having difficulty paying your bills.

Note any financial stressors: _____

☐ **Emotional stressors.** *Example:* You continually find yourself feeling depressed and worried about all sorts of things; or you suffer from low self-esteem and are continually putting yourself down.

Note any emotional stressors: _____

☐ **Change stressors.** *Example:* You recently changed jobs, moved into a new house, and are expecting your first child. (Even when changes are positive, they can be sources of stress.)

Note any change stressors:_____

☐ **Other stressors:** _____

_____

Sometimes it helps just to identify the sources of your stress. At least, then, you know what you're dealing with. With the sources categorized like this, you may be able to think of ways to change your situation so that you'll be subjected to less stress.

If you can't change anything about your situation, you can still change your response to it. One of the primary ways to change your response to stress is to learn to relax. In the next section, we'll show you a variety of methods designed to help you relax. (There are entire books written on this subject. As a supplement to the methods outlined here, you may want to refer to at least one of these books. We'll list the two that we've found most helpful at the end of this chapter.)

Managing Stress by Learning To Relax

You can learn to counter the physical effects of stress: the best tools for doing so are relaxation techniques. When we talk about relaxation in this context, we are not simply referring to relaxing activities, such as listening to music or reading a book. Rather, we will focus on specific techniques which have been proven to have certain positive physiological effects on your body, including a decrease in heart rate, blood pressure, and muscle tension. You already learned one type of relaxation exercise, paced breathing, in Chapter 5. Paced breathing is particularly well suited to managing acute anxiety. The techniques we describe below are best for lowering chronic levels of stress.

To start with, we'll go over one of the most widely used relaxation techniques.

Progressive Muscle Relaxation

Since Progressive Muscle Relaxation (PMR) was first developed in 1929 by Dr. E. Jacobson, considerable research conducted by Drs. D. Bernstein and T. Borkovec has demonstrated the technique's effectiveness. In fact, PMR is the best researched and probably the most well known of the anxiety management techniques. PMR involves systematically tensing and relaxing various muscle groups. When you tense each muscle group, you focus on the feeling of tension. Then, when you allow the muscles to relax, you focus on the contrast between the tension and the relaxation. This technique provides you with the physiological benefits of relaxation, as well as improving your ability to recognize tension when you feel it. By increasing your awareness of tension, PMR can help you pinpoint the muscle groups that are your trouble spots—the places where you experience the most tension—allowing you to relax them before you become too anxious.

Before describing PMR in more detail, a word of caution is in order. People with back or neck problems may want to skip the sections in which you tighten those muscles. Also, don't tighten your muscles too strenuously, especially while you are just learning the technique.

You can try PMR by following the instructions below. You may want to tape-record the instructions while you're first learning, so that you don't have to continually refer to this book while you're trying to practice the technique. There are also many books that include detailed scripts you can follow. After a while, you'll memorize the routine, and won't need a tape (it's probably best not to be overly reliant on a tape anyway, as your ultimate goal is to be able to relax anywhere at anytime).

To try PMR, first find a comfortable place to sit or lie down. Rate your anxiety level before you begin by using the 0-10 scale we introduced in Chapter 5. You'll be able to monitor your progress by rating your anxiety level both before and after your practice sessions.

Here's the basic procedure to follow with each muscle group:

1. Begin with a deep, abdominal breath. You may want to silently say the word "relax" as you breathe slowly out.

2. Next, separately tense the individual muscle group.

3. Hold the tension for about five-to-ten seconds.

4. Then, release the tension slowly.

5. Take another deep breath and silently say "relax" as you breathe slowly out.

Now, using the above procedure, here are the major muscle groups to focus on. Do each step sequentially. Remember to breathe first, tense the individual muscle group, hold, release, then take another breath.

Your head

1. Clench your teeth and pull the corners of your mouth back in a forced smile.

2. Close your eyes tightly.

3. Open your eyes as wide as you can.

Your neck and shoulders
(Omit if you have neck problems)

1. Press your head to your right shoulder, then your left.

2. Press your chin toward your chest.

3. Tilt your head towards your back (but not too far).

4. Raise your shoulders up toward your ears in a big shrug.

Your arms and hands
(Can do right and left sides separately)

1. Tighten your hands into fists.

2. Tighten the muscles in your upper arm by making a fist and bending your arm up at the elbows.

3. Press your hand firmly into the surface where you're practicing.

Your chest and lungs

1. Take a deep breath and puff out your chest.

2. Tighten your chest muscles.

Your back
(Omit if you have back problems)

1. Arch your back.

Your abdomen

1. Push your abdomen out as far as you can.

2. Pull your abdomen in tight towards your spine.

Your hips, legs, and feet
(Can do right and left sides separately)

1. Tighten your buttocks.

2. Push the soles of your feet down into the floor (press your heels if you're lying down)

3. Point your toes downward.

4. Flex your toes upward.

Autogenic Relaxation

The term *autogenic* refers to something produced without external influence or aid—in other words, something you can do by yourself. Developed by Drs. J. Schultz and W. Luthe, this relaxation technique began as a combination of hypnosis and self-suggestion. In their present form, autogenic exercises are a means of helping you teach your body to respond to your verbal instructions. This form of relaxation differs from PMR in that no muscle tensing is involved. Instead, you use the power of your mind to change how your body reacts to stress. The basic technique involves concentrating on various parts of your body and allowing those muscles to relax. Learning to respond to various verbal cues is also an important part of this technique. These verbal cues instruct you to notice particular sensations, such as feelings of warmth and heaviness in your muscles.

Below are some instructions for autogenic relaxation. Remember to rate your anxiety level both before and after you try this method.

An autogenic relaxation exercise. Begin by sitting or lying down comfortably. Start with three deep breaths and allow yourself to begin to relax. Then, focus on your left hand. Become aware of how your left hand feels. Tune in to the sensations there. As you allow your hand to relax, you notice it feeling slightly warmer. Say to yourself, "My hand is feeling warm and heavy." Allow this warmth and relaxation to flow all throughout your hand. After a while, you can notice this comfortable warmth spreading up into your wrist and forearm. Gradually, it flows up past your elbow and into your upper arm, then up into your shoulder as well. Say to yourself, "My arm and shoulder are feeling heavy, warm, and relaxed." Take a few moments to notice the feelings of relaxation.

If you want to give autogenic relaxation a try, you can repeat the above instructions for each of the major body areas we listed above for PMR. You can also intensify the feelings of warmth by forming pictures in your mind. For example, you might want to imagine the sun shining down on your body as you practice this technique. Again, the two books we mention in the recommended readings section at the end of this chapter contain full autogenic relaxation scripts.

Imagery Relaxation

A third type of relaxation involves the use of imagery. This relaxation technique is different from PMR and autogenics, in that you focus primarily on a scene rather than on your body. For example, many people find the beach to be a very relaxing place.

Here is a sample "mini"-script for an imagery relaxation exercise. You might want to record this script on an audio tape. Before you begin the exercise, take a moment to jot down your anxiety level.

An imagery relaxation exercise. Imagine that you are walking along a beautiful, uncrowded beach. You can feel the warmth of the sun as it shines down on your head and shoulders. Just notice how soothing that warmth can feel. You can hear the sound of the waves as they come in... and go out...in and out. With each breath you can smell the slight scent of salt in the air, and the air feels clean and refreshing. With each breath you feel more calm, more relaxed, and more in control. After a while, you find a comfortable spot on the beach and you lie down. As you look up in the sky, you notice how blue it is. Eventually, a large puffy white cloud floats slowly across the sky. Imagine what it might feel like to float effortlessly on that cloud...

This is just one example of what you can do with imagery. You can devise your own scene that will be pleasantly relaxing for you. The images you pick can be from a vacation you've had, or stolen from a relaxing fantasy. Common examples that people select for relaxation imagery involve scenes in the woods, lying on a raft in a swimming pool, taking a nap in a hammock, relaxing in a meadow, sitting by a stream. The best scenes to use are those you can imagine quite vividly. Concentrate on all the details and use all your senses to complete the picture. As you look around, what's there? Where are you in relation to other things in the image? Are you sitting or standing? What do you hear? What is the temperature like? What do you smell? How do you feel? What else do you notice about your surroundings? Be sure to take your time when practicing imagery, so you can get the full benefits of relaxation.

Imagery relaxation techniques aren't for everyone. If you don't have a vivid imagination, you may find practicing this method tedious and difficult. That's okay. Simply select another method from the ones we've suggested, or from the many others you can find in other books. However, if you enjoy this type of relaxation and practice the skill, you'll be able to take a vacation in your mind whenever you begin to feel anxious.

Managing Stress through Other Lifestyle Changes

In addition to learning a relaxation technique, you may also want to make changes in your lifestyle to combat stress. First of all, examine your diet. One often overlooked but important factor that contributes to anxiety and stress is caffeine. How much caffeine do you consume each day? Be sure and consider all the sources. Although coffee is often the biggest offender, there are many other sources of caffeine in the American diet, including tea, cola drinks, and chocolate. Caffeine can make you jittery and nervous. If you consume a lot of caffeine, you may want to try to cut back gradually and see how you feel. Be sure and make the switch slowly! Going "cold turkey" often results in a nasty headache.

Also look at your general eating habits. If you're skipping meals, eating at irregular times, or stringently dieting, you're doing yourself a disservice. Erratic eating plays havoc with your blood sugar levels. This, in turn, can affect your moods and contribute to increased bodily symptoms of anxiety.

How much sleep do you get? You're bound to feel groggy, jittery, or not quite yourself if you don't get enough sleep.

Finally, think about whether you're getting regular exercise. Even though it can be rough getting yourself to the gym or to go for a walk, exercise is a proven stress fighter. Be sure and check with your doctor, though, before beginning a new exercise program.

Making even one of these changes toward a healthier lifestyle can go a long way towards helping you manage stress more effectively.

Summary

Sometimes stress can interfere with your ability to fully recover from a social phobia. Although you can't eliminate stress from your life, you can learn to manage it more effectively. The first step is to identify the sources of your stress. Next, you can learn specific relaxation techniques and make other lifestyle changes to help you feel more comfortable and in control of your life.

Recommended Reading

Charlesworth, E.A. and R.G. Nathan (1984) *Stress Management: A Comprehensive Guide to Wellness.* New York: Atheneum.

Davis, M., E.R. Eshelman, and M. McKay (1988) *The Relaxation and Stress Reduction Workbook.* Oakland, CA: New Harbinger Publications.

13

What If I Have
Other Problems?

For many of you, carefully following the methods outlined in previous chapters has led to a substantial reduction in your social fears. If this has been your experience, you may not need this chapter. Others, however, may have found recovery more difficult. Sometimes, lack of progress is caused by the presence of another problem. If this is your situation, read on. This chapter will discuss some of the more common emotional or interpersonal problems that can complicate recovery from a social phobia. Let's begin by talking about depression.

Depression

Everyone feels down in the dumps from time to time. For some people, however, feeling depressed becomes a major complication, which can prevent adequate recovery from a social phobia. In a study conducted in 1990, researcher Dr. Murray Stein and his colleagues found that 35 percent of individuals with social phobias had experienced at least one "major depressive episode." What exactly does this mean? Some of the symptoms of a major depressive episode include

- Depressed mood (feeling "blue")

- Decreased interest or pleasure in daily activities

- Sleep disturbances (either sleeping too much or too little)

- Appetite disturbances (again, eating too much or too little)

- Fatigue

- Decreased concentration

- Feelings of worthlessness

What are some of the reasons why individuals with social phobias become depressed? There are several possible explanations. Sometimes the social phobia itself causes, or at least contributes to, depression. Everyone needs a certain amount of social interaction to feel happy and content. If you don't get enough "people contact," it's natural to feel sad and lonely. If you have been avoiding a wide variety of social situations, and your life has become more and more restricted, depression would not be an uncommon response. Most likely, as you begin to address your social fears and become more comfortable in social situations, your depression will lift.

Another explanation for why people with social phobias may become depressed relates, once again, to maladaptive thinking—or, as one person so aptly called it, "stinking thinking." Chapter 6 went over in detail how your thoughts can contribute to your anxiety. In a similar manner, your thoughts also can contribute to your feeling depressed.

Let's go back to Amy, the woman who couldn't urinate in public restrooms, whom we mentioned in Chapter 1. Amy blamed herself for having such a "stupid" problem. During one therapy session, she exclaimed in frustration, "There's so many world problems and here I am worried about whether I'm going to be able to urinate or not! I'm so dumb!"

It's important to remember that no one chooses to have a social phobia any more than one chooses to have diabetes, for example. Both are very real problems, deserving of careful attention and treatment. Beating up on yourself serves no useful purpose; it only keeps you stuck in a depressed and hopeless state. Amy's negative thoughts didn't stop with the above criticism. She also believed herself to be a total failure as a person, just because of this one problem area. She discounted all of her positive contributions and focused instead on her difficulty using public restrooms. One of the frequent elements in her self-talk was "I'm hopeless. I'll never get any better." This thought was quite distorted. Despite making considerable progress in her exposure therapy, she minimized her accomplishments, choosing to focus on how far she still had to go.

There's yet another explanation for why some people with social phobias become depressed. Sometimes depression, or feeling hopeless, can be one more form of avoidance. This type of avoidance can sometimes be difficult to recognize, because you feel genuinely depressed, not as if you're avoiding anything!

So, how does this avoidance strategy operate? Try and think back to your own experiences with exposures so far. When doing planned exposures, did you ever feel kind of down, as if you just didn't have enough energy to complete the task? Or as if it were useless to try? "What if this exposure therapy stuff is a bunch of baloney?" you may have asked yourself. Before long, you may have talked yourself out of doing the exposure. "I'll do it tomorrow, when I feel better."

Are you beginning to see how this kind of depressed attitude is actually another form of avoidance? Rather than facing the anxiety you will experience when doing exposures, it sometimes feels easier, or more familiar, to give up: to feel hopeless instead. Although this reaction is certainly understandable (no one enjoys feeling anxious!), it does you harm in the long run. It is even more important to carry out your planned exposures on the days when you feel bad. If you wait for your mood to change before you act, you may wait for a long time. Almost always, if you go ahead and get moving with something you're putting off, you'll feel better afterwards. Sometimes just being aware of this kind of avoidance can be enough to keep it in check.

Finally, it's possible that both depression and anxiety disorders, such as social phobia, share some underlying contributing factors. You may be vulnerable to both types of problems for the same reason, whether this is an inherited biological predisposition, or environmental factors that have influenced the development of both these disorders.

Other Tips for Dealing with Depression

There are several other suggestions for dealing with depression. First of all, make sure that you are giving yourself credit for your accomplishments, no matter how small they may seem. The only way to change behaviors is step by step. No matter how small those steps may seem to you, they are, nonetheless, very important. If you have difficulty recognizing all you have done, think about making a list of your accomplishments. Refer to this whenever you start focusing exclusively on how far you have left to go. It's okay to look ahead to your goals, but it's equally important to praise yourself for all the hard work you've done.

You may even want to set up some kind of system of rewards for yourself. For example, Jennifer was having difficulty recognizing her accomplishments, so she set up a very simple but effective reward system for herself. Every time she completed a planned exposure, she gave herself a point. After she earned five points, she did something nice for herself. None of her rewards involved spending a lot of money. They were just simple, pleasurable activities, such as taking a bubble bath or going for a walk on a nearby nature trail. This reward system actually served several functions for Jennifer. Not only did she start realizing that she was making progress towards her goals, but she also benefitted from learning to treat herself with kindness— something she had never done before. You might experiment with a reward system for a couple of weeks to see if you notice any benefits. Refer to Chapter 14 for more details on setting up such a system.

It's also helpful if you're feeling depressed to make sure that you are relatively active throughout the day. Some people may spend a significant amount of time in bed when they're depressed. A vicious cycle can develop in which you feel depressed, and then become even less active. The less active you are, the more depressed you feel. If you are having difficulty breaking out of this cycle, write out a daily schedule by the hour, or even the half-hour, of what you will do when, and then stick to it! This will seem very difficult at first, but it's enormously useful. Just like Jennifer above, you can also use a point system to give yourself credit for each hour during which you did what you planned. Schedule a few walks around the neighborhood or a nearby park. Exercise is a great depression fighter. Research has shown that aerobic exercise (in which your heart rate is elevated for at least 20 minutes) causes endorphins to be released in the brain. Endorphins are the body's natural pain killers and can generate a sense of overall well-being and relaxation.

If you find that even after following the suggestions in this section your depression does not improve, please consider seeking professional consultation. If you are feeling so low that you have thoughts of hurting yourself or taking your life, you *definitely* need to contact a mental health professional right away. We discuss how to find professional help in Chapter 17.

Substance Abuse

Another problem that can complicate a social phobia is substance abuse. Some people with social phobias have found that alcohol or drugs alleviate some of their anxiety, and oftentimes, alcohol is readily available in the social situations most feared. Research conducted by Dr. F. Schneier and his colleagues found that 16 percent of people with social phobia also have a problem with alcohol abuse. Furthermore, the social phobia almost always began before the problem with alcohol.

What does this mean? Most likely, people with social phobias feel terribly disabled by their anxiety, and sometimes don't know where to turn for help. These people may have unwittingly discovered that alcohol or other drugs calmed them down. Gradually, they develop a pattern of using alcohol or drugs to "self-medicate" their social phobic symptoms. This can be a particularly troublesome complication to deal with. Not only do you have the original social phobia, but now you also have an equally difficult problem of substance abuse to overcome.

So, what problem do you deal with first? In our experience, it is difficult to help someone with a social phobia if he or she is still abusing alcohol or other drugs. Alcohol and drugs cloud your judgment and perceptions, making any type of psychotherapy more difficult. This may be especially true for exposure therapy. Remember that the way exposure therapy works is by helping you habituate to the bodily symptoms of anxiety, and disproving your catastrophic thoughts. If you are abusing alcohol or drugs, you don't have the opportunity to find out that you can handle your anxiety and other symptoms in the social situations you fear. Consequently, the therapeutic effects of exposure cannot take place. It is for this reason that we recommend that you deal with the substance abuse first, or at the very least, you should address this problem at the same time you are working on your social phobia.

One possible way to tackle substance abuse problems is to attend Alcoholics or Narcotics Anonymous (AA or NA) meetings. You can probably find a listing in your phone directory for these organizations. AA and NA are self-help groups where people with similar problems go to support each other in trying to live a life free of alcohol and drugs. An alternative group that is becoming popular in many parts of the country is Rational Recovery, a self-help group based on the principles of cognitive therapy. If you muster the courage to go to any one of these meetings, you'll probably meet other people who have suffered with social anxiety and used alcohol or drugs in attempts to deal with their problem.

Granted, for some people with a social phobia, going to a support group is probably the last thing they feel able to do. However, the process may be worth the effort, and deserves consideration.

Another option is to see a professional who specializes in substance abuse. You could call your local chapter of the National Council on Alcoholism and Drug Abuse for names of qualified professionals. If you do see a substance abuse professional, be sure and tell him or her that you also have a problem with social anxiety. However, please note that many drug and alcohol treatment programs do not adequately attend to the needs of someone with a social phobia. You may need to seek out a therapist who has worked with anxiety disorders after you have completed treatment for your drug or alcohol problem.

Other Anxiety Disorders

Individuals with a social phobia can also have another anxiety disorder. There are several kinds of anxiety disorders besides social phobia, each with its own set of complications. We briefly describe them below. If any of these descriptions seems to fit you, you may want to seek professional consultation or read more about the disorder you feel you have. We have listed some related readings at the end of the chapter. Unfortunately, space limitations prevent us from outlining ways to cope with all of these problems within this book.

Panic Disorder and Agoraphobia

People with panic disorder have frequent panic attacks (described in Chapter 2) that often seem to come "out of the blue" and are not easily linked to one type of situation (for example, social situations). A person's fear of these attacks can lead him or her to avoid any situation that might trigger them (such as driving, crowds, being alone). When panic attacks lead to this sort of persistent avoidance, the condition is known as *agoraphobia*. Dr. David Barlow, an anxiety disorder expert, found that 17 percent of individuals with social phobia have an additional diagnosis of panic disorder and agoraphobia.

Obsessive-Compulsive Disorder (OCD)

Obsessive-compulsive disorder can be extremely debilitating. People with OCD experience intrusive and disturbing thoughts that cause severe anxiety. In order to deal with this anxiety, they often feel the need to perform some type of repetitive act, called a ritual or compulsion. For example, if someone obsesses about contamination or germs, he or she might engage in excessive handwashing. Other types of common rituals include excessive checking (such as whether the stove is off or the door is locked), counting, and hoarding. These rituals can consume many hours each day. Results from Dr. Barlow's research showed that four percent of individuals with social phobia also have OCD.

Generalized Anxiety Disorder (GAD)

People who have generalized anxiety disorder worry about many areas of their life. Common areas of concern include health, family, finances, and work. While everyone worries from time to time, people with GAD feel unable to "turn off" the worry, and the worry greatly interferes with their life. They are also likely to develop physical symptoms of anxiety as a result of continually being upset. It is not uncommon for individuals with social phobias to have a general tendency to worry as well. In fact, Dr. Barlow found that eight percent of socially phobic individuals also have GAD.

Post-Traumatic Stress Disorder (PTSD)

Post-traumatic stress disorder can result after someone has experienced a traumatic event such as sexual or physical assault, a severe accident, or a war. Symptoms of PTSD typically include nightmares and *flashbacks*, which are intrusive images or recollections of the traumatic event. People suffering from PTSD often go to great lengths to avoid "cues" that trigger painful memories or emotions connected to the traumatic event. For example, someone who develops PTSD after being raped in a car may avoid riding in cars altogether. Such people often experience depression as part of their disorder. Symptoms of PTSD may come on immediately following the trauma, or may be delayed for months or even years.

Simple Phobia

The term *simple phobia* refers to a fear of something quite specific. For example, people with simple phobias may fear flying or heights, dogs, bee stings, or blood. Simple phobias are extremely common, and often do not pose a problem. It is probably less likely that a simple phobia would interfere with recovery from a social phobia than some of the other anxiety disorders listed above.

Relationship Problems

Human beings are most comfortable and secure when their world is stable and predictable. When change occurs, people often feel unsettled, especially at first. What will these changes mean for me? Will I like these changes? Will I be able to handle them? Sometimes change—even positive change—can be so disconcerting that people try and avoid it.

What does this mean for you, someone working to overcome a social phobia? And what does this mean for the people who care about you?

If you are working to make changes in your life, people close to you are inevitably going to have reactions to these changes. Not all of these reactions will be helpful for your recovery. Let's take Gail's situation to illustrate this point. She was working at being more assertive as one component of her plan to overcome her social phobia. She had always been so fearful of disapproval that she never dared say what was on her mind, not even to her husband. In the past, she never questioned anything he did or said, nor did she say what she wanted or needed. As Gail gradually began to risk being assertive, her husband, Richard, was a bit uneasy with the changes. This was especially so because Gail was just learning assertiveness skills, and they were not terribly polished yet. Sometimes, her anxiety level crept up, and she came across as critical or demanding.

Richard felt a bit threatened. And who could blame him? He had become used to a wife who never disagreed with him. In the early stage of Gail's recovery, he sometimes lashed out in anger at her. "What's wrong with you—you're so critical all the time! Can't I do anything right anymore?" Comments such as these would often lead to an argument, leaving both of them feeling discouraged. For a while, Gail felt like giving up. Maybe overcoming her social phobia and becoming more assertive wasn't worth it.

With a lot of patience and hard work on both their parts, they were able to work through this difficult period. Gail kept practicing her assertiveness skills, and learned to express her opinions and ask for what she wanted in a way that didn't put Richard on the defensive. Richard learned that Gail's progress could also benefit him: he didn't have to guess what she wanted anymore; and, as she continued to overcome her social phobia, they could do more things socially.

Even though getting used to the changes in Gail was scary at first, he loved Gail and ultimately was pleased that she was gaining a new sense of herself as a strong and independent person. He felt that their relationship was growing stronger as Gail grew to be more confident. Their relationship had a solid yet flexible foundation that could weather the process of change.

Although your situation is probably different from Richard and Gail's, the point is that change can be challenging for both parties involved—but it can be achieved. People have a remarkable ability to adapt to new circumstances. In the next section, we have outlined some tips for significant others interested in learning more about how they can be helpful in supporting your recovery. Ask your spouse, family member, or any other interested party to read these guidelines.

Although no research has yet explored the effectiveness of marital or family therapy for treating social phobia, it makes sense that such treatment methods will be helpful for some individuals. Couples therapy promotes better communication skills, which can allow people to feel more at ease in a variety of social situations. In addition, less stress at home creates a better environment in which to work on your social phobia.

Tips for Family Members or Significant Others

If someone you care about has a social phobia, here are some general guidelines that may help you navigate through his or her recovery.

Caring about someone who has any type of anxiety disorder can be challenging. You may have made many sacrifices in attempts to be understanding of your loved one's problem. For example, you may turn down invitations to social events because you know that he or she would be anxious in such a situation. It is natural for you to have felt angry or resentful at times. After all, you're missing out on a lot of fun and the company of someone you care about. It's helpful to remember to get angry at the behavior rather than at the person. This can be a difficult distinction to make, especially when you're mad; however, it's important. Attacking someone's character or "personhood" can be very harmful to their self-esteem. This doesn't mean that you can't state how you feel. For example, you could say, "I really want to go to the picnic and I'll miss your company," or even, "I feel angry and disappointed when I have to go to social events without you." The important thing to remember is to express your own feelings as *I*-statements (I feel this, I wish that), rather than attributing your feelings to the other person's behavior (You make me feel...). Also try and understand that the person with the social phobia is not acting this way to hurt or punish you. If you take phobic behavior as a personal rejection, it will only compound the problem. Refer to Chapter 11 in this book for more guidelines on *I*-statements and healthy communication skills.

Research has shown that when people are attempting to learn new behaviors, they respond much better to support and positive reinforcement than to criticism. Just as we have continually reminded the person with the phobia, we want to remind you to focus on the person's accomplishments, no matter how small they seem. You can also ask the person how you may be of most support. Don't offer false reassurance; but do remind your loved one that you will continue to love them, regardless of how an exposure turns out, regardless of whether they make a mistake or incur another person's disapproval. Even if you disapprove of a particular behavior, your love is unwavering.

You may need to monitor your own behavior to make sure that you aren't unwittingly reinforcing your loved one's avoidance strategies. Sometimes even well-intentioned behavior is actually harmful (in the language of codependence theory, it's called *enabling*). For example, if you always answer the phone because you know that talking on the phone is difficult for your loved one, you are enabling his or her fears to continue, and making it even less likely that he or she will find a solution. This kind of enabling behavior is very easy to understand. You may have witnessed your loved one's extreme anxiety in social situations before; and, naturally, you don't want to see him or her suffer unnecessarily. And yet, for improvement to occur, a phobic person must experience the anxiety in order to work through it. Although this may seem like unkindness or cruelty in the short run, this strategy will be vastly more helpful in the long term; and you will be a much better friend!

Summary

Complications can arise during the treatment process. Concurrent psychological disorders—such as depression, substance abuse, and other anxiety disorders—can make recovery from a social phobia more difficult. It's best to address these problems directly. Sometimes, despite your best efforts, these complicating factors may require outside assistance from a mental health professional.

Recommended Reading

Bourne, E.J. (1990) *The Anxiety and Phobia Workbook*. Oakland, CA: New Harbinger Publications.

Copeland, M.E. (1992) *The Depression Workbook: A Guide for Living With Depression and Manic Depression*. Oakland, CA: New Harbinger Publications.

Foa, E.B., and R. Wilson (1991) *Stop Obsessing: How to Overcome Your Obsessions and Compulsions*. New York: Bantam Books.

Steketee, G., and K. White (1990) *When Once Is Not Enough: Help for Obsessive Compulsives*. Oakland, CA: New Harbinger Publications.

Wilson, R. (1986) *Don't Panic: Taking Control of Anxiety Attacks*. New York: Harper & Row.

14

What If I Need
Greater Incentive?

In Chapter 4 we recommended that you ask yourself, "What reason do I have to change my reaction to disapproval?" We believe the answer to this question to be very important. The strength of the reasons that influence your decision to overcome a social phobia can determine whether or not you are successful. Your reason to recover creates the incentive you need to work hard on your problem. Without proper incentive, you're unlikely to follow through with your recovery plan.

If you do lack incentive, don't be too discouraged. In this chapter, we describe ways to increase your incentive and, in so doing, your chances for a successful recovery. First, let's take a look at what we call your long-term incentives.

Long-Term Incentives

If you look at your list of reasons for recovery in Chapter 4, you will probably find that most of these can be classified as long-term incentives—things that you want to see happen in the future, once your phobia has lessened. These are the really big reasons for dealing with a social phobia: to have a better life, make more friends, go to college, meet someone to marry, and so on.

If you have no long-term incentives, or the ones you have don't seem very important, you've got a problem. Unless your weak incentive is strengthened, you are unlikely to devote the time and energy necessary for recovery from a social phobia.

What if you don't have any long-term goals you can think of? What if you just don't know what you want to do? It has been our clinical experience that very few people have absolutely no long-term interests,

goals, or aspirations. Many people, however, simply don't allow themselves to think about long-term incentives, because it makes them anxious,
or they have given up on the hope of ever changing their life. Identifying
long-term incentives requires you to be willing to fantasize, daydream,
and dwell on the things in life you truly desire—things you cannot have
or do now because of your social phobia.

In this next exercise we would like you to write down your list of
reasons for recovery again. Only this time, you must write down any
reasons that come to mind, even if they make you feel anxious. Please
do not censor items on the list because you feel they are out of your
reach, or for any other reason. Think of this as a wish list.

Reasons To Recover from My Social Phobia:

My Long-Term Incentives

1. _____
2. _____
3. _____
4. _____
5. _____
6. _____
7. _____
8. _____
9. _____
10. _____

If you were having trouble coming up with reasons before, we hope
that this last exercise helped you think of additional reasons for recovery.
Take a look at the items you wrote down. Are they important to you?
Do you feel as if they will motivate you to pursue recovery? We hope
you answered yes to both of these questions.

With your long-term incentives in place, you may feel better about
your chances for overcoming your social phobia. However, beware! Even
with several strong long-term incentives, your day-to-day commitment to
recovery can falter. Long-term incentive is often not enough by itself. Below we'll discuss another kind of incentive that may give you the added
boost you need.

Immediate Incentives

There is another, very different kind of motivation that can contribute to your recovery. This consists of immediate, or short-term, incentives. Unlike long-term incentives, immediate incentives are neither grand nor lofty, but rather are much more humble in their scope. They're very much akin to the gold stars you may remember from kindergarten or first grade: of negligible value materially, but highly-prized nonetheless.

Although immediate incentives may not be as impressive as long-term incentives, they do have one definite advantage: they do not happen next month, next season, or next year. The gratification that comes with them comes immediately.

So what are these immediate incentives? They are the simple pleasures of life you can use to reward yourself for a job well done. For example, money can serve as an immediate incentive. You might promise to pay yourself $2.00 for every exposure you successfully complete (and then to spend the money on something special that's just for you). There are countless other possibilities for short-term incentives: rewarding yourself with leisure time; participating in a fun activity; treating yourself to a favorite snack; making long-distance phone contact with an old friend; going to the movies; taking time out to listen to music; taking a long, hot bath; going out to your favorite restaurant; buying yourself something new. Notice that all these examples are things that you can, to some extent, control. In other words, you can decide how, when, and if to administer your reward. As you will see, this is a very important feature of immediate incentives.

Immediate incentives can help you overcome your social phobia by creating daily motivation in a way that long-term incentives cannot. Take Nora's situation for example. Nora works for a medium-sized advertising agency doing copywriting. One of the items on her long-term incentive list is to be able to go into business for herself. She has school-age children and she wants to be home when they get out of school in the afternoons. Doing freelance work would allow her the flexibility she wants. But starting her own business would involve meeting with clients and selling her ideas to them—something she's never been comfortable doing. She knows that she'll have to overcome her fear of making presentations before she can fulfill this dream. Nora incorporates the use of immediate incentives into her recovery plan. Each time she completes an exposure, she puts a set amount of money into a special savings account—money she eventually plans to use to start her business. Watching the balance in her account accumulate offers Nora tangible evidence of her progress, and the encouragement she needs to keep going.

Immediate incentives can help motivate you to do the things on a day-to-day basis that need to be done in order to achieve your long-term goals.

Now take a minute to think about some immediate incentives you might apply to your recovery plan. Remember—a useful incentive should be something you can realistically afford or arrange to do, and that you personally enjoy or find rewarding. This can be an object, an activity, or an event, as long as it is something you feel will motivate you. After you have thought about some immediate incentives for your recovery plan, write them down in the spaces provided below.

Reasons To Recover from My Social Phobia:

My Immediate Incentives

1. _____
2. _____
3. _____
4. _____
5. _____
6. _____
7. _____
8. _____
9. _____
10. _____

Using Incentives in Your Recovery Plan

Now that you have identified your immediate incentives, it's time to decide how you will use them to promote your recovery. You do this by making incentives contingent on a particular accomplishment. This simply means that after you have accomplished a step in your recovery plan (practiced paced breathing, performed an exposure) you recognize your accomplishment by rewarding yourself with one of the incentives you've chosen. Receiving that particular reward becomes contingent on completion of a specified segment of your recovery plan (for example, treating yourself to a restaurant meal every time you do an exposure). Making incentives contingent on a particular action follows a very basic principle of behavioral science—when a difficult behavior is followed by a pleasant event you increase the probability of the difficult behavior being repeated.

Using incentives to promote a desired behavior is not a new idea. Most of us go to work each day, in great part, because we are paid to do so. Entertainers like to perform, in part, because of the applause and adulation they receive. However, most people do not use incentives intentionally to overcome such difficult behavioral or psychological problems as social phobia. It takes effort to think of incentives and figure out how to use them. Also, some people feel embarrassed or discouraged at the idea of having to use incentives to get themselves to do things they "should want to do naturally." They don't realize that there is no reason why anyone *should* want to do something unpleasant. And yet it helps to create immediate incentives in the pursuit of any goal. They can provide one more source of motivation to face the unpleasantness of the task at hand.

It's now time to add immediate incentives to your recovery plan. Use the form below to outline your recovery plan for the coming week (make photocopies of the page to use for the weeks to follow). First, decide what exposures or other recovery plan activities you will perform this week, and write them in the column labelled "Activity." Second, designate the time and date of each activity and write them in the appropriate columns. Finally, decide which incentive you will receive for each activity, and note this in the column labelled "Incentive."

This Week's Recovery Plan Schedule

Date	Time	Activity	Incentive

Summary

Weak incentive is a common reason why some people don't accomplish their recovery goals. There are two kinds of incentives. Long-term incentives are the major reasons you want to overcome your social phobia. Immediate incentives, on the other hand, are less significant, but can have a powerful impact on your ability to follow through with your recovery plan on a day-to-day basis. Immediate incentives can be integrated into your recovery plan. They provide extra motivation to perform the tasks necessary to deal with your social phobia.

15

How Do I Maintain My Progress?

We've done a lot of talking in this book about change. One more important thing to know about change is that it does not always continue uninterrupted. Progress toward overcoming your social phobia will entail steps forward as well as steps going in the opposite direction. It's to be hoped that your steps forward will far outnumber the steps you take backwards. You should know that setbacks are common in this type of therapy, even expected. While no one enjoys a setback, the important thing to remember is that they do not have to escalate into a total relapse: an extended or permanent return of your old fears of disapproval. Keep in mind that you can sometimes learn just as much from a setback as from your steps forward!

What Is a Setback?

Put simply, a setback is a noticeable increase in your fears of social situations after you've begun to progress toward overcoming your phobia. An increase in fear may not be the first thing you notice. Sometimes the first sign is a change in your behavior. Take Jane, for example. She had made great strides in overcoming her fear of eating in public, when, one day, a friend asked her to join her at a nearby restaurant for lunch. Jane liked this friend and really wanted to see her. But instead of accepting the invitation, she made an excuse for why she couldn't go. This was the first signal that Jane's fear was returning.

Less obvious behaviors may also signal a setback. Bob, for example, had worked hard to become more comfortable attending large social gatherings. Then, for no apparent reason, he found himself drinking much more than usual at a class reunion. This represented a setback for him.

You may be thinking that we're making a big deal out of nothing. Perhaps Jane just wasn't in the mood to go out to lunch. Maybe Bob simply felt like "having a good ol' time" that night. Granted, there may be a variety of explanations for Jane and Bob's behavior. However, any sign of increased avoidance in the face of your social phobia could point to a setback that needs prompt attention.

Why Do Setbacks Happen?

There are a variety of reasons why setbacks occur. Sometimes, they happen when you're under increased physical or mental stress. For example, if you've been sick with the flu, your resistance may be lowered, leaving you more susceptible to fatigue and anxiety. Physical stress can leave you with less mental energy to combat maladaptive thinking. In addition to illness, other kinds of stress—such as work or family problems—may exacerbate social anxiety. This is particularly true if the stress caused you to feel less confident in some way.

Setbacks don't just occur when life is rocky, however. You can experience a setback after a period of success—a time when you'd least expect a problem. A setback after good times can really catch you off guard. Under these circumstances, a setback may mean that you've become complacent. Thoughts such as, "It's sure nice to relax and ignore this social phobia problem," and "I'm glad I don't need to do exposures anymore," may signify such an attitude. In a booklet on relapse prevention, author Judi Hollis makes an apt analogy. "The tightrope walker, so well practiced he almost performs while sleeping, is the one facing slips and near misses. The newly trained aerialist or acrobat exhibits stringent caution...It is the seasoned performer, lulled into false confidence, who takes the fall." Although it's essential to feel proud of your accomplishments, you can't maintain your gains without continually confronting your social fears.

Preventing Setbacks from Becoming a Relapse

Setbacks are not by themselves cause for great alarm. One setback is usually not a big deal. However, when setbacks become frequent, and more the rule than the exception, you may be headed for a relapse.

Almost all relapses can be prevented. The important thing is to try and head relapses off at the pass by dealing with setbacks effectively as they arise. Here's how to do it.

1. Identify the Warning Signs

Before you can prevent a relapse, you need to identify your own set of warning signs. Here are some common examples of warning signs to look for:

- An increase in physical symptoms of anxiety when you find yourself in a previously feared social situation.

- An increase in distressing maladaptive, automatic thoughts.

- An increase in avoidance behavior, including partial avoidance.

- Development of new, or worsening of old, problems, such as depression or substance abuse.

- An increase in time spent worrying about what other people will think of you.

2. Determine Which Recovery Steps You've Stopped Practicing

Once you've identified the warning signs, the next step in warding off a relapse is to determine which recovery steps you've stopped practicing. Perhaps you initially found paced breathing to be an effective tool for managing your physical symptoms of anxiety; but you haven't been practicing lately, much less implementing this skill on a daily basis. What about challenging your maladaptive thinking? Have you become lax in keeping a thought record, and evaluating whether you're exaggerating the probability or severity of disapproval? Consider your use of exposures. Are you challenging yourself to confront feared social situations on a regular basis, or have you fallen into old patterns of avoidance? Also consider other recovery steps you may have let slide. Was stress management a part of your recovery plan? Do you need additional practice with social skills? What about using incentives to keep yourself motivated? Make a list of the recovery steps you need to start practicing again.

3. Develop a Relapse Prevention Plan

Next, determine specific actions you'll take once you notice any warning signs. Referring to your list of recovery steps you need to start practicing again should help you know how to proceed.

For example, you may want to increase the number of exposures you are doing, or begin doing them again if you've stopped altogether. You might want to make a point of practicing and using your paced breathing more routinely. In addition, it wouldn't be a bad idea to keep a record of your thoughts again: use the rating scales in Chapter 6 to evaluate your estimates of probability and severity of disapproval. If you were working with a therapist, consider scheduling a "booster session." You and your therapist can then work together to get you back on track.

In addition to planning specific actions you will take, think of specific coping statements to deal with the potential relapse situation. Many people feel a sense of panic or doom at the first sign of relapse. Thoughts such as "Oh no, I'm failing again!" or "This is awful, I can't take this again!" can lead you into a cycle of hopelessness. Rather, you need to remember that it's normal to experience setbacks, and that relapses occur sometimes despite the best intentions. This is not a time to berate yourself! Instead of heaping criticism on your head, simply tell yourself that something has gone wrong that you need to correct. Then take action!

It's a good idea to get your plans down on paper in the form of a *relapse prevention plan*. We'll use Tom, the police officer with the fear of public speaking to see what a relapse prevention plan might include.

Tom's Relapse Prevention Plan

Warning Signs:

1. Making no comments in a department meeting for more than two weeks in a row.

2. Persistent, increased physical symptoms of anxiety when talking in front of others.

3. Increased worry about what others are thinking about me during meetings.

4. Increased stress in other areas of my life that I'm not handling well. [When Tom got bogged down with other problems, his pattern was to withdraw and become increasingly quiet.]

5. Feelings of depression.

Recovery Steps I've Stopped Practicing:

1. I've stopped doing exposures on a regular basis.

2. I haven't practiced my paced breathing in a while.

3. I haven't been monitoring and evaluating my thoughts.

Specific Steps To Carry Out:

1. Begin regular, planned exposures until symptoms improve again.

2. Practice anxiety management skills daily.

3. Keep thought diary again and use rating scales to evaluate probability and severity distortions.

4. Talk this problem over with my wife, rather than trying to hide it and pretend that everything's fine.

5. If danger signs continue for two months with no sign of improvement, I will contact a mental health professional.

Coping Statements To Help Prevent Relapse:

1. Just because I'm falling back into my old patterns right now doesn't mean I'm a total failure. I can still get back on track.

2. I can learn from this experience.

3. It's good to confront my fears.

4. It's okay to make mistakes. Nobody's perfect.

Composing Your Relapse Prevention Plan

It's now time to develop your own personalized relapse prevention plan. This is a very important step in your recovery. You may think that you'll naturally know what to do if you find yourself headed for trouble; but take our word for it that it helps to have a well-thought-out plan written down ahead of time. Keep a copy of this plan in a place where you can refer to it easily.

My Relapse Prevention Plan
(Post this in a prominent place!)

Warning Signs:

1. _____
2. _____
3. _____
4. _____
5. _____

Recovery Steps I've Stopped Practicing:

1. _____
2. _____
3. _____
4. _____
5. _____

Specific Steps To Carry Out:

1. _____
2. _____
3. _____
4. _____
5. _____

Coping Statements To Prevent Relapse:

1. _____
2. _____
3. _____
4. _____
5. _____

What If a Relapse Occurs?

Despite people's best intentions, sometimes a relapse does occur. In fact, you may be reading or rereading this book after experiencing a relapse. If so, you are to be congratulated on having the courage to start again. The first step back to recovery is to accept the fact that yes, you have relapsed, but no, it's not the end of the world. The most important thing is to not criticize yourself for slipping back; remember that you did the best you could at the time.

You can probably get back on track more quickly than you'd expect. Many times, people who have relapsed are able to return to their pre-relapse status faster than they did the first time. After all, you've already learned the necessary recovery skills once. It's mostly a matter of reviewing what you already know, and beginning to do exposures again. If you carefully assess what led to your relapse and make plans for dealing with similar situations in the future, your recovery can be even stronger than before.

Summary

Setbacks are a common part of the process of change. When setbacks become frequent or prolonged, however, you may be headed for a relapse: an extended or permanent return of your old fears of disapproval. Fortunately, relapses can be prevented. Preventive measures include making a list of warning signs to look for, knowing what recovery steps you've stopped using, and developing a plan of action, including specialized coping statements to mitigate the effects of setbacks and prevent them from escalating into a relapse.

16

What If I Need Medication?

At some point, you've probably said to yourself, "I wish there was some medicine I could take to make this problem go away." In fact, you may have already discussed your symptoms with a physician who perhaps recommended medication. You were then faced with a decision: "Should I take a drug for my social phobia?"

This is a difficult decision to make without first knowing the advantages and limitations of various drug treatments. The purpose of this chapter is to provide basic information about medications that are currently available to people with social phobias. We hope that this information will help you work more effectively with your physician as you consider your medication options.

Decisions about medication are made even more difficult by conflicting opinions within the professional community. Mental health professionals who believe that social phobia is solely the result of a biochemical irregularity might tell you that the only answer is medication. However, there are others who will describe your problem as arising from environmental causes. Some of these professionals might discourage you from considering medication under any circumstances. We take a more moderate view.

We have found that some socially phobic individuals recover without medication; but, for others, drugs can be quite helpful. Medication, when used properly, is one of several valuable tools to help relieve the physical symptoms of anxiety. If you think back to our explanation of the origins of social phobia in Chapter 2, you'll recall that we stressed that a combination of biological and environmental factors can influence your social phobia. As a result, a combination of strategies might be necessary to help you recover. Taking either extreme position—being afraid to take medication under any circumstance, or seeing drugs as the only effective treatment—will interfere with your ability to consider all your options for recovery, and could leave you short-changed.

What You Should Consider Before Taking Medication

There are two obvious decisions you and your physician must make before you take medication. First, should you take medication at all? And second, which drug should you take once you decide to take medication? In this section, we will address the first question by discussing the advantages and limitations of medication, and by outlining some of the situations in which drugs can be helpful.

Advantages of Medication

There are several advantages to taking medication. Compared to all of the work involved in overcoming a social phobia using cognitive and behavioral techniques, it requires little effort to take a prescribed drug. Taking an easier approach may be particularly appealing if your problem with social phobia presents itself infrequently. In addition, medication is widely available. There are many psychiatrists and other physicians who are able to treat your problem with medication. In contrast, psychotherapists, particularly well-trained behavior therapists with expertise in treating social phobias, may not be as accessible in your community as physicians who can prescribe medication. Finally, in some cases drugs can reduce specific physical symptoms, such as rapid heart rate or shaking, that bother people with social phobia.

Limitations of Medication

One of the limitations of taking medication is that it may provide you with a means for avoiding symptoms associated with the fear of disapproval. As you have read throughout this book, we don't encourage you to avoid your fear. Rather, you can only overcome what you fear by confronting it and learning to manage the anxiety that accompanies it. For example, taking a medication may help you sweat less; but, at the same time, it's important that you learn to tolerate some sweating. If your goal in taking medication is to continue avoiding unpleasant symptoms, we encourage you to examine your motives. True, it's easier to open a bottle of medicine to cope with anxiety than follow all of the steps we've outlined. But as far as we know, taking medication alone, without making any changes in how you think about your fears, will only temporarily reduce or relieve your symptoms.

A second limitation is that taking medication doesn't teach you skills or provide self-confidence. Relying solely on medication may leave you vulnerable to relapse, particularly if you stop taking the drug before you've acquired the skills necessary to combat your social phobia.

The third drawback concerns side effects. Without learning other ways to cope with social anxiety, you may end up taking medication indefinitely—and, frankly, the long-term effects of these medications are unknown. In addition, some people have difficulty with the short-term side effects of medication. For these people, the side effects are worse than the potential benefits of staying on the drug.

When Is Medication Indicated?

The combination of medication, along with the cognitive and behavioral techniques outlined in this book, may be your best chance to overcome the fear of disapproval. Dr. Stewart Agras from Stanford University School of Medicine believes that it makes good clinical sense to treat social phobia both pharmacologically and psychologically. However, not everyone needs to take medication in order to recover; and, as you now know, there are advantages and disadvantages to drug treatment. The decision to take medication should be made on an individual basis and in consultation with your physician.

You may be asking yourself, "When is the right time for me to consider medication?" The symptoms of anxiety you experience while either anticipating or entering social situations are the usual targets for medication-based treatment. As we mentioned above, there are definitely appropriate circumstances in which to think about discussing medication with your doctor: if the situations in which you experience social anxiety occur very infrequently; if you are having trouble getting through even the lowest-ranked items on your hierarchy because your symptoms are so distressing; if your anxiety aggravates a neurological problem, such as a tremor; or if your level of anxiety is so high throughout the day that you feel consistently miserable.

It's also time to think about medication if the methods outlined in this book just aren't working. This doesn't mean that you're a failure, but rather that the type of treatment approach we've suggested simply isn't right for you. It could also mean that you've run into a roadblock in your treatment that you can't handle on your own. If this is the case, you may want to take a look at Chapter 17 which deals with finding professional help. In the meantime, consider the option of medication.

To summarize, the following are times when taking a medication may be indicated:

- You want to try a double-barrelled approach: medication and cognitive-behavioral techniques.

- You seldom encounter situations in which you fear disapproval, and feel that medication is the easiest, most effective option.

- You're having difficulty completing even the easiest exposures on your hierarchy due to anxiety.

- You're having continuing difficulty coping with physical symptoms of anxiety (such as, rapid heart rate, sweating, trembling, and so on) despite using anxiety management skills.

- You've run into a snag in treatment that you can't seem to overcome on your own, or the methods we've outlined aren't working for you by themselves.

Drug Treatments for Social Phobia

In this section we will address the issue of which drug to take once you've decided to take medication. Some of the drugs we describe have been tried as a targeted treatment for social phobia, while other drugs have been used with other types of anxiety and are not specifically designed to combat social fears. Although there is limited research supporting the use of medication to treat social phobia, drugs have been shown to be effective in treating some specific performance anxieties. In fact, there have been several studies of a group of medications called beta-blockers (which will be described below) that have reduced performance anxiety among musicians, athletes, and college students. Another group of medications, the monoamine oxidase inhibitors (MAOIs, which are also described below), are showing increasing promise in the treatment of more generalized forms of social phobia. Preliminary studies suggest that three kinds of drugs—beta-blockers, MAO inhibitors, and benzodiazepines—may be effective in the treatment of social phobia. Let's take a look at each of these groups of medications in more detail.

Beta-blockers

You may have first heard about beta-blockers from a friend who has a heart condition, high blood pressure, or chest pain. If your doctor has suggested a beta-blocker to help reduce your symptoms of anxiety, it's not necessarily because he or she thinks that there's something wrong with your heart. Rather, beta-blockers reduce what are commonly referred to as peripheral symptoms of anxiety (for example, rapid heart rate, flushing, and sweating). Among the more commonly prescribed beta-blockers for the treatment of social phobia are propranolol (*Inderal*) and atenolol (*Tenormin*).

As we noted above, beta-blockers have been found to be most effective for the treatment of very specific performance anxieties. In fact, the peripheral symptoms we listed are frequently seen in people with stagefright. It's in just this kind of situation where beta-blockers seem to do the most good.

How beta-blockers work. It's thought that in performance situations, the autonomic nervous system is aroused. This state of arousal then increases social anxiety. The beta-blockers or, as they are more accurately called, the beta-adrenergic blocking drugs, work by blocking certain nerve cell receptors (the beta receptors). These nerve cells are located within the autonomic nervous system. As the name implies, beta-blockers such as propranolol (*Inderal*) and atenolol (*Tenormin*) block the beta receptors, thus reducing symptoms such as increased heart rate, blood pressure, and tremor. As a result of taking one of these medications, a patient's anxiety-related symptoms of increased heart rate, sweatiness, or shaking hands may be reduced.

Dosage. For those of you with specific social phobias, the beta-blockers can be taken one of two ways. According to Dr. Agras, a single, "as-needed" dose of the medication can be taken previous to a feared social encounter (for example, giving a speech). The aim, in this case, is to use the medication to reduce the beta-receptor-related symptoms of anxiety. This reduction in symptoms indicates that the autonomic nervous system is sufficiently blockaded. Ten-to-forty mg of propranolol to be taken 45 to 60 minutes before the feared situation is frequently prescribed by physicians to reduce physical symptoms of performance anxiety.

If you will be encountering phobic situations on a more regular basis (for example, you may have to give talks or be in meetings on a daily basis), a beta-blocker can be given as a daily, scheduled dose. In their *Physician's Handbook*, experts from the American Psychiatric Association indicate that atenolol is often prescribed in doses between 50 and 100 mg per day. The medication reaches its therapeutic level in approximately two weeks.

Side effects. The most common side effects from taking a beta-blocker are fatigue and weakness. In some cases where dosage has not been properly adjusted, blood pressure and pulse can drop too low. While not as common as these side effects, but nonetheless disturbing, depression and impotence have also been known to occur. Generally, these side effects can be avoided by fine-tuning the dose of the medication to the particular individual's needs.

Coming off the medication. As with many of the medications used to treat anxiety, you should not attempt to adjust your dosage of a beta-blocker by yourself. This includes stopping the medication. If you decide that it is time for you to begin to handle anxiety-producing situations without the aid of medication, discuss this issue with your prescribing physician. You will need to be on a schedule to help you gradually taper off the beta-blocker.

Who shouldn't take beta-blockers. If you have certain medical conditions, beta-blockers are not for you. If, for example, you have a history of bronchial asthma, congestive heart failure, or certain kinds of cardiac arrhythmias (such as bradycardia) or conduction abnormalities, you may need to consider another medication. Be sure to discuss these issues with your prescribing physician.

Monoamine Oxidase Inhibitors (MAOI)

Although studies of the use of MAO inhibitors to treat social phobias are limited, they are beginning to grow more numerous. At the 1991 conference of the Anxiety Disorders Association of America, the MAO inhibitors were given increasing amounts of attention for the treatment of the generalized form of social phobia.

Historically these drugs have been found effective in the treatment of depression. Dr. Michael Liebowitz, a well-known researcher in the area of anxiety disorders from Columbia University College of Physicians and Surgeons, has noted that, in patients with one form of depression, MAOIs reduce interpersonal sensitivity, which can be viewed as one measure of the fear of disapproval.

Studies have indicated that the MAOI phenelzine (*Nardil*) has been helpful in reducing situationally cued anxiety. Unfortunately, many of these studies not only included socially phobic individuals, but agoraphobic individuals as well, making it difficult to draw any definite conclusions. However, Dr. Leibowitz and his colleagues have presented interim data from an extensive study of socially phobic subjects. Thus far, they have concluded that phenelzine was more effective for the generalized form of social phobia, while atenolol, a beta-blocker, was more effective for treating the more specific social phobias.

How MAOIs work. These drugs act to block or inhibit the action of a particular enzyme—monoamine oxidase. The MAOIs were first used to treat tuberculosis and were found to have the effect of elevating the mood of those patients suffering from this lung disease. The medication was then tried with depressed psychiatric patients, with similar results. MAOIs were first used the the 1960s with anxiety-disordered individuals who had what we now call panic attacks.

The MAOIs are thought to act by affecting the availability of certain chemicals in the sympathetic part of the central nervous system. As we have pointed out in earlier chapters, the arousal of the sympathetic nervous system causes certain neurotransmitters to be released, resulting in a "fight-or-flight" anxiety response. While it takes a period of a few weeks for the next step to occur, the MAOIs cause the receptor sites for these arousing chemicals in the sympathetic nervous system to be "down-regulated"—the sites, in effect, become less receptive to these particular neurotransmitters and thus compensate for their overabundance in the system. In addition, certain neurotransmitters themselves (norepinephrine and epinephrine) are deactivated by MAOIs, which also helps to reduce the arousal of the sympathetic nervous system. The MAOIs, then, are thought to help prevent an anxious overreaction to otherwise nonthreatening events.

Dosage. Although there are several MAOIs available, the one most frequently prescribed and studied is phenelzine (*Nardil*). Dr. Agras and other experts note that dosages of up to 90 mg per day have been found to help reduce social anxiety. As we noted in the preceding paragraph, adjustments that the MAOIs are thought to make in your nervous system take time. Thus, it can take up to four weeks for the medication to exert its therapeutic effect.

Side effects and precautions. Some physicians dislike prescribing MAOIs because a strict dietary regimen must be adopted. Not only must this diet be adhered to while you are taking the drug, you must also be careful for two weeks after you stop. Foods high in tyramine must be eliminated from your diet. The following list is not exhaustive, but foods high in tyramine include: meats prepared with tenderizers; smoked or pickled fish; beef or chicken liver; sausages; canned figs; bananas and avocados; cheese and all foods containing cheese, such as pizza (although cottage cheese and cream cheese are allowed); yogurt; sour cream; beer, red wine, and other alcoholic beverages; soy sauce; yeast extract (Brewer's yeast); excessive amounts of coffee or chocolate; and any foods that have been aged, pickled, fermented, or smoked. All decongestants, hay fever, and sinus medications must be discontinued, as should asthma inhalers and any form of stimulant.

You may be thinking that it's probably alright to cheat a little on this kind of diet. But cheating on this kind of diet won't put on pounds; it will land you in the emergency room with a potentially life-threatening crisis. The combination of an MAOI and tyramine first results in a sharp throbbing headache which then ushers in a rapid elevation in your blood pressure that is called "hypertensive crisis." If caught in time, a doctor can administer medications which will reduce your blood pressure back to normal. What is important to keep in mind is that if you think an MAOI will be of help to you, you must be willing and able to stick to the dietary and medication restrictions that your doctor will outline in greater detail.

More common side effects of the MAOIs include a lowering of blood pressure that may be particularly noticeable if you change position quickly. These changes in posture often result in feelings of dizziness or faintness. Other side effects include drowsiness, stomach or intestinal distress, appetite changes, muscle twitching, restlessness, and sexual difficulties. Usually an adjustment in the dose of your medication can alleviate these side effects. Additional side effects can include severe chest pain, enlarged pupils, severe headache, increased sensitivity of the eyes to light, nausea and vomiting, stiff or sore neck, unusually rapid or slow heartbeat, or unusual sweating.

Coming off the medication. Unlike the beta-blockers or the benzodiazepines, there are fewer problems associated with your withdrawal from the MAOIs. You will still have to follow your physician's directions with regard to stopping this or any other medication. It is important to remember that you will have to continue to avoid foods high in tyramine for two weeks after you discontinue the medication.

Who shouldn't take MAOIs. You shouldn't take an MAOI if you are already on a tricyclic antidepressant. This is a potentially lethal combination of medications. If you have chronic asthma and have need of an inhaler, the MAOIs are not for you either. Likewise, if you have a history of problems maintaining a normal blood pressure (if your blood pressure is either high or low), you will need to discuss the choice of this medication thoroughly with your doctor. Given that the MAOIs interact with several other prescription as well as over-the-counter drugs, if you need any other medication, this will have to be discussed with your doctor before you can consider taking an MAOI.

Benzodiazepines

The third group of medications is a relative newcomer as a specific treatment for social phobia. These drugs are most often referred to as anti-anxiety medications and include several compounds with which you may already be familiar. For example, the benzodiazepines include such medications as diazepam (*Valium*) and chlordiazepoxide (*Librium*), as well as newer drugs such as alprazolam (*Xanax*) and clonazepam (*Klonopin*). Other brand names you may have heard about include *Tranxene, Ativan, Centrax,* and *Restoril.*

Currently, alprazolam *(Xanax)* is among the most researched of the benzodiazepines that have been used to treat social phobia. In addition, three recent case studies by Dr. Jeffrey Davidson and his colleagues from Duke University Medical Center suggested that clonazepam (Klonopin) may also be an effective medication. Preliminary data from case reports, as well as on-going clinical trials, indicate that alprazolam may be beneficial for some people who suffer from social phobia. There are no known controlled studies of any of the other benzodiazepines, such as clonazepam, for the treatment of social phobia.

Dr. Agras has concluded that in pharmacologically treating a generalized social phobia, an MAO inhibitor should be tried first; if it doesn't work, a benzodiazepine might be tried. Clinically, we have found that, despite the effectiveness of the MAOIs, many of the people we see in our clinic are reluctant to try them because of the dietary restrictions and possible side effects. For some of these individuals, a benzodiazepine is quite helpful in assisting them to overcome their initial symptoms of anxiety so that they can become more actively engaged in cognitive-behavioral therapy.

How benzodiazepines work. The benzodiazepines have five clinically useful effects. Of primary interest to us is their anxiety-reducing property. They also act as a sedative-hypnotic (in other words, a sleeping pill), can help reduce seizure activity, function as a muscle relaxant, and can be used as a preanesthetic medication. These drugs bind to a very specific receptor site on the nerve cell—the benzodiazepine receptor. These receptors are widely distributed throughout the central nervous system. The benzodiazepine receptor is intimately connected to a major inhibitory neurotransmitter system in the brain of mammals. As a result, the benzodiazepines work in concert with this inhibitor neurotransmitter, called gamma-aminobutyric acid (GABA). GABA is estimated to be present at 40 percent of the nerve cell junctions in the brain. Due both to the prevalence of GABA and the high affinity of benzodiazepines for GABA binding sites (that is, the benzodiazepine receptor), these receptors were found to have an important role in how the GABA junction worked. The current theory holds that these particular nerve cell junctions are important for anxiety modulation.

Dosage. Many physicians prescribe *Xanax* or related benzodiazepines on an "as-needed" basis (in other words, you only take them when you feel anxious). In some cases, this is an effective approach. However, we encourage you to discuss with your physician the possibility of prescribing benzodiazepines on a schedule (say, three or four times a day), especially if you anticipate feeling social anxiety during a good part of the day. If you are taking medication on demand to deal with anxious moments, it may detract from your ability to use your coping skills, and could lead to your concluding, "I can't get through this without my pills." Instead, a regular dosing schedule provides a constant level of the medication in your system to help you combat anxious moments without your needing to take a pill whenever you get anxious.

Most physicians will start you on a low dose of a benzodiazepine like *Xanax*, and gradually increase your dose. The American Psychiatric Association recommends that the initial dose of *Xanax* range from 0.25 mg to 1.00 mg. Most people will begin to feel a reduction in their overall level of anxiety with doses in the 1-6 mg range.

Side effects and precautions. The most common side effect of the benzodiazepines is drowsiness. It's for this reason that you're started on a low dose, since you will gradually overcome the drowsy feelings. Obviously, until your body adjusts to the medication, you'll need to be careful or refrain from activities requiring alertness, quick judgment, coordination, and fast reaction time (such as driving or operating heavy machinery). At higher doses, you may simply feel slowed down. Other less commonly occurring side effects include dizziness, headache, muscle weakness, fatigue, dry mouth, nausea, and skin rash. These medications may also cause menstrual irregularities, and may affect sexual functioning.

You may have read newspaper articles, or heard on television or radio programs, opining that the benzodiazepines are addictive. Although all of the benzodiazepines have the potential for abuse, dependence, and withdrawal reactions, they are far less hazardous than barbituates or alcohol. It's true that a physical and sometimes psychological dependence develops as a natural course of taking the medication. However, unless you have a history of abusing drugs or alcohol, the dependency issues can usually be managed effectively when the medication is prescribed properly and you are adequately prepared and informed. Be sure to discuss these issues thoroughly with your prescribing physician.

Coming off the medication. Withdrawal from the benzodiazepines should be achieved in consultation with your physician. For some individuals, particularly those who are on a high dose of these medications, withdrawal can be a problem if it occurs abruptly. Symptoms of benzodiazepine withdrawal include insomnia, irritability, increased anxiety, panic attacks, stomach and intestinal upset, palpitations, headache, muscle aches, confusion, and possibly seizures. These symptoms are easily avoided by having the medication tapered off gradually. We cannot emphasize this enough: *consult your physician if you are taking benzodiazepines and wish to stop.*

Who shouldn't take benzodiazepines. If you are pregnant, intend to become pregnant, or if you're breast-feeding, you generally shouldn't take a benzodiazepine. As we've already mentioned, if you have a history of alcohol or other chemical dependency, you're not a good candidate for these drugs either. The benzodiazepines can occasionally cause problems with breathing in people with chronic, progressive lung problems (such as emphysema), sleep apnea, or other respiratory disorders. Some of the benzodiazepines are not recommended for use by older adults and/or persons with liver damage or kidney disease. If you are taking any other medication, it's critical that you inform your prescribing physician, because the benzodiazepines may interact with that medication. (For example, *Valium* is not recommended if you're taking *Dilantin* or digoxin.) If you frequently have need for antacids, they'll interfere with the effectiveness of benzodiazepines. Because of their sedative effects, benzodiazepines are to be taken with caution and only after you've consulted with your physician—especially if you are already taking opiates, tricyclic antidepressants, antipsychotics, alcohol, antihistamines, barbituates, or other sedatives.

Other Drug Treatments for Anxiety

The three types of medication we've described are not the only medications used to treat symptoms of anxiety. There are at least two other groups of medications that are commonly prescribed. Although these medications haven't been used extensively to treat social phobia, they've been used with other types of anxiety and could eventually prove useful as a treatment for this disorder. Because of this, we will briefly describe these two groups of medications, the tricyclic antidepressants (TCAs) and the azaspirones.

Tricyclic Antidepressants (TCA)

The TCAs have been used for quite some time in the treatment of other anxiety problems, such as panic disorder and agoraphobia. The most extensively studied of the TCAs for the treatment of these disorders is imipramine (*Tofranil*). Generally, it's been found that for many individuals with panic disorder and agoraphobia, imipramine provides effective symptom relief.

The TCAs work by blocking the reuptake of certain neurotransmitters, making these chemicals more available for the receiving nerve cells to use. Some of the common side effects of TCAs include blurred vision, dry mouth, constipation, and urinary retention. Unfortunately, many people who are anxiety prone find these temporary side effects to be distressing and, as a result, have difficulty tolerating the medication.

Azaspirones

The more accurate pharmacological name for this group of medications is azaspirondecanediones. A drug called buspirone (*Buspar*) is the most studied of this relatively new family of medications. The advantage of this drug is that it has a low potential for abuse, and causes relatively few side effects. While *Buspar* is often considered instead of a benzodiazepine for its ability to reduce symptoms of anxiety, it doesn't have many of the other properties of the benzodiazepines (such as their anticonvulsant, sedative, or muscle relaxant effects). The mechanism by which buspirone exerts its effect is unknown.

There are mixed reports as to the effectiveness of this medication for the treatment of any condition besides generalized anxiety. At a recent panic awareness training seminar, Dr. Jerrold Rosenbaum, the Chief of the Clinical Psychopharmacology Unit at Massachusetts General Hospital, called into question the usefulness of buspirone for the treatment of panic. He also noted that this medication was even less effective if a patient had been previously treated with a benzodiazepine. In contrast, at the 1991 National Conference on Anxiety Disorders and in the *Journal of Clini-*

cal Psychiatry, Dr. Michael Liebowitz reported that, in an uncontrolled study, several socially phobic individuals experienced an improvement in symptoms with buspirone. He did, however, note that buspirone did not seem to be as potent as the MAOI phenelzine for the treatment of social phobia.

At this point, it seems premature to recommend buspirone for the treatment of social phobia, since controlled research has yet to support its effectiveness for anything except generalized anxiety.

Summary

Once again, we return to a point made earlier. Our knowledge about social phobia is in its infancy. As a result, researchers are still looking for the proverbial "silver bullet" when it comes to finding an effective medication to treat social phobia. In some instances, medication may be sufficient. For those of you who decide to take a drug, it is more likely that a combination of medication and cognitive-behavioral therapy will be necessary, particularly if your anxiety is so high that you need medication to reduce your physical symptoms to the point where you can maximize the effectiveness of therapy. You should become familiar with the advantages, limitations, and proper uses of medication. We have provided some guidelines and general information to help you feel more comfortable discussing these issues with your physician.

17

How Do I Find
Professional Help?

By now, we hope you're well on your way to overcoming your social phobia. But if you've gotten stuck somewhere in the process of trying to help yourself, you're not alone. Although some people can recover on their own, others need the assistance of a trained professional. There's no shame in asking for help. The only shame is when people who need treatment don't get it, continuing to lead their lives in misery. In this chapter, we'll go over some of the reasons why it may be a good idea to seek professional consultation, as well as how to select a therapist.

Deciding When It's Time To Seek Professional Help

Several times throughout this book, we've pointed to problems you may face during the recovery process which might require professional help. Let's review and summarize some of these "red flags" before continuing.

One of the first problems you may have encountered was in setting your goals. Perhaps in completing the self-assessment you found out that you're fearful of such a wide variety of social situations that your goals would have to include "everything." This was the case for John, a 33-year-old accountant who had a generalized social phobia. He was afraid of talking in meetings, giving work-related presentations, introducing himself, going to parties, and even speaking casually with his neighbors. When he wrote out his list of goals, he felt overwhelmed. He hadn't the slightest idea about what to work on first. At first, John felt defeated. He had hoped to work through this problem on his own. He wasn't used to asking for help. But he knew that he needed some professional guidance in planning a realistic recovery program. For John, mustering the courage to seek professional help was the best thing he could do for himself. With the assistance of a trained therapist, John was able to determine which goal to work on first. This step was important: he didn't want to start with too ambitious a goal and end up feeling even more overwhelmed and discouraged.

Although it may be more common for someone like John, with a generalized social phobia, to require professional help, there are also several instances when someone with a specific social phobia may decide to seek therapy. If you have a specific social phobia (such as a fear of writing in public or using a public restroom) you may feel unnerved at the idea of completing your first few exposures on your own. You may think to yourself, "If I could do what I'm afraid of, I wouldn't have this phobia in the first place!" In many ways, you're right. The techniques outlined in this book can be extremely challenging, to say the least. Sometimes people benefit from the support and guidance a therapist can provide in the difficult process of facing their fears. More specifically, many may benefit from what is called "therapist-assisted exposure," especially during the early phases of the recovery process. Perhaps an example will help illustrate how this process can work.

Marlene is a 66-year-old retired widow who sought treatment for a specific social phobia—fear of signing her name in public. Her husband, who had previously handled all of their business and financial matters, had recently died. On top of the natural grief she was feeling, Marlene was also faced with the daunting fact that she would have to overcome her fear. There were numerous papers to sign related to the estate. Besides that, she would have to learn to write checks or sign credit card receipts in public in order to manage her everyday life. Marlene knew that she wouldn't be able to overcome her fear on her own, so she sought the assistance of a therapist. But when her therapist explained the technique of exposure, Marlene was shocked. Surely there was an easier way! She had so many catastrophic thoughts. What if her hand started shaking in front of the bank teller? Wouldn't she make a complete fool of herself?

Her therapist suggested that, as a first step, they go together to a nearby bank. While at the bank, the therapist went to the first available teller window. Marlene discreetly stood back a bit, but was fully able to see and hear what was going on. While at the window, the therapist pretended her hand was shaking so much that she was unable to sign a check. She even grabbed the shaking hand with her other hand and exclaimed, "I just don't know what's wrong with me today. I can't seem to get my hand to quit shaking." The teller was very kind and patient and told her to take her time. Finally, the therapist was able to sign her name, but apologized for her messy writing. The teller assured her that the bank didn't care about neatness. Later, Marlene and her therapist discussed the experience. Marlene was surprised at how the teller reacted. Seeing her therapist go through with the exposure had chipped away at some of Marlene's distorted thoughts about what would happen if her hand shook. In fact, watching her therapist do the exposure gave her the courage to try a similar exposure herself.

This is just one example of how a therapist-assisted exposure might work (not all therapists are accustomed to working in this manner). There are many variations. You're only limited by your own and your therapist's creativity in designing exposures to confront your particular fears. Many people find that once they've completed a few therapist-assisted exposures, they're ready to tackle exposures on their own.

In addition to the reasons for seeking professional help we've just discussed, there are several others. Many of these were described fully in Chapter 13, so we'll just list them here for a quick review. You should consider seeking professional help if

- You are significantly depressed for more than a few weeks at a time.

- You have any thoughts of hurting or killing yourself or someone else.

- You are experiencing problems with substance abuse.

- You think you may have another anxiety disorder as well.

- You're finding that you have a lot of relationship problems—perhaps as a result of your social phobia, but not necessarily so.

- You've made progress in overcoming your social phobia, but you're experiencing a relapse and can't seem to get back on track.

Choosing a Practitioner

Once you've decided to consult a mental health professional, you're faced with yet another decision—whom to call. Unfortunately, the mental health profession doesn't make this choice easy for you. There are psychologists, psychiatrists, social workers, psychiatric nurses, counselors, and the ubiquitous "therapists," all of whom have different kinds of schooling. To make matters worse, even within a particular professional group, practitioners' level of specialization in the treatment of anxiety disorders can vary widely. We'll first briefly describe the differences between the various categories of mental health professionals, and then mention training and specialization.

The Different Kinds of Mental Health
Professionals—Which to Choose?

The bad news is that there's no one right choice when it comes to deciding on a mental health professional. No matter what anyone says is best, you have to believe that you can effectively work with a particular individual. There are competent and incompetent practitioners in mental health, just as in every other profession. The good news is that there are increasing numbers of professionals who are specialists in the treatment of anxiety disorders. What this means is that, in many metropolitan areas, if you don't quite hit it off with one person, there are apt to be others you can choose among to get specialized treatment for your problem. You just have to figure out where to start.

To begin with, many people are confused when you have to choose between a psychologist and a psychiatrist, since both usually have the title "doctor." The easiest way to distinguish between the two professionals is that psychiatrists are physicians and, therefore, are able to prescribe medication; whereas psychologists are doctors of philosophy (or of psychology) and are trained primarily in how to deliver such psychological services as psychotherapy. Other therapists—such as social workers, psychiatric nurses, and counselors—usually have masters degrees in their area of specialization. All of these professionals may know how to conduct psychotherapy. However, it is important for you to know the specifics regarding the education and training of the professionals you've contacted, and whether they are licensed to practice.

So how do you know if your psychotherapist has the skills required to treat social phobia? Although it seems altogether too simple, you have to ask! Many consumers are concerned that their questions about background and training will offend professionals. In our experience, most mental health professionals are not put off by being asked to discuss their credentials. In fact, most therapists expect to be asked questions about their training. When it comes to decisions about childcare, most parents take great pains to interview prospective babysitters. Why should you do any less when it comes to trusting someone with your own care? Perhaps, then, the cardinal rule in selecting a mental health professional is to *ask questions.*

Finding a Professional Who Is Knowledgeable
about Social Phobia

Over the past decade, more and more centers for the treatment of anxiety disorders have been established nationwide. Not only do many of these centers treat anxiety disorders, including social phobia, but they often offer advanced training for mental health professionals in the treatment of these disorders. Most often, these specialists have completed one to two years of advanced training beyond their degree.

Not all of those who specialize in the treatment of anxiety have completed their training at anxiety disorder centers. There are several centers that offer training in cognitive-behavioral therapy; and there is ample research supporting these approaches as effective treatments for anxiety disorders. Thus, many of the professionals who have completed additional training in cognitive-behavioral therapy have also been trained in the treatment of anxiety.

While it's an obvious plus if a professional was trained at the kind of center described above, this is not the only route to learning to treat social phobia. Since these training centers have not been in existence for very long, some professionals may have deliberately sought other forms of training to augment their skills. For example, they may have attended seminars or workshops on the treatment of social phobia. Or they may have received supervision from someone else who has experience in treating social phobia.

Not every mental health professional has the training needed to work with people who have social phobia. You need to ask for specific information about what kind of training a practitioner has received. Some other questions you might want to ask include how many people with social phobia they've treated and how successful their treatment appears to be. Some practitioners can also arrange for you to speak with someone they've worked with who had a similar problem. Keep in mind, though, that ethical practice dictates that practitioners protect the confidentiality of the people they treat; so it may take a little organizing and some time to honor this kind of request. Ask for the information that will allow you to feel good about investing your time, energy, and money.

Where Do I Find Help?

To find a qualified mental health professional, you need to be a good consumer. Contact resources in your community, such as a university medical center or an anxiety disorders treatment center, and ask about the kind of treatment that's available. Programs based in a university medical center are more likely to stay current with those treatments that are most effective for treating anxiety disorders. Such programs are frequently listed in the yellow pages of your telephone book in the "Hospitals" section.

If you live in a community in which this kind of facility is unavailable, calling the nearest university medical center or anxiety disorders treatment center, and asking for a referral to someone in your community, may yield some useful information.

Another alternative is to contact the Anxiety Disorders Association of America (301/231-9350), your local Mental Health Association, or the licensing boards of the various mental health professionals in your state (which are often located in the state capitol). Any one of these resources may be able to provide you with information as well as the names of practitioners in your area who specialize in the treatment of anxiety disorders or cognitive-behavioral therapy.

Another resource you may have overlooked is friends or relatives who have been in therapy. Ask friends who have been treated for a problem with anxiety and find out if they were satisfied with their treatment. A friend, or even a friend of a friend, may be able to give you the name of a professional who was able to help. Word of mouth is an excellent means of discovering resources. One final word of advice. Once you've begun treatment, you should feel increasingly more comfortable working with that professional as time passes. If, for some reason, you and your therapist are not hitting it off, discuss your concerns with him or her. After all, in therapy as in other relationships, not every match is made in heaven. Your concerns may be something that the therapist can address. If things don't improve, your therapist should be able to help you find another professional with whom you will be able to work successfully.

Summary

There are several reasons to seek professional help, including difficulty defining your goals and feeling overwhelmed with the seeming enormity of the task at hand. In addition, we discussed the value for some people of doing therapist-assisted exposures. We also listed several other reasons to consider seeking professional help, such as depression or coexisting anxiety disorders. The remainder of the chapter focused on different categories of professionals who treat social phobia, and the kinds of training you can expect them to have. We emphasized the need to be a good consumer in locating a professional who will be most beneficial.

18

Some Final Comments: Future Directions

We hope that the preceding chapters have helped you become familiar with social phobias. You've learned that they're a common but sometimes debilitating problem. You've read about the nature of social phobias and the various ways in which they interfere with people's lives. You've also learned about some possible causes of social phobia, and that the fear of disapproval is shaped by how you think, feel, and behave. Most importantly, you've learned ways to overcome social phobias. In covering this material, we've tried to provide the latest information available. Yet much is still unknown about this disorder. In these final pages we'll discuss some important unanswered questions about social phobias—questions which we hope will be addressed by future research.

How Do Social Phobias Relate to Other Disorders?

We still need to learn more about how best to define and classify social phobias. As we mentioned in Chapter 1, there is nothing sacred about the current definition of social phobia or the way in which it is now classified among the anxiety disorders.

It can be argued that social phobias should be placed in the same category as other phobias, since they have so many things in common. And yet, social phobias are in some ways unique. Additional research is needed to decide whether social phobias should be classified separately from other types of anxiety problems (is fear of disapproval fundamentally different from fear of snakes, heights, or thunderstorms?).

On the other hand, not all social phobias are alike. It's possible that specific social phobias, such as the fear of eating in public, should be classified separately from generalized social phobias that affect so many aspects of life. Even specific social phobias differ from one another. Fear of public speaking, for example, is ten times as prevalent as other types of social phobia, and much less likely to involve psychological distress. Should fear of public speaking be classified separately from other specific social phobias?

These issues may seem overly technical, and irrelevant to your own problem. However, the way in which a disorder is defined and classified is very important. For instance, it can affect whether or not your phobia is easily identified by your doctor or therapist, and whether or not you receive the right treatment. You may have already had the distressing experience of having a professional incorrectly diagnose your problem as a medical condition, or attribute it completely to stress. If you had such an experience, it's unlikely that you benefitted much from that professional's advice. The frustration and disappointment that result from misdiagnosis can be reduced in the future as a more precise definition of social phobia evolves.

What Causes Social Phobia?

Questions about how to define and classify a disorder can be partially answered by gaining a good understanding of its causes. Unfortunately, as you learned in Chapter 2, our understanding of the causes of social phobia is not yet complete. Theories have only begun to be developed and researchers have just recently turned their attention to social phobias (unlike some of the anxiety disorders, which have been more extensively studied). Learning about the possible role of biochemistry, heredity, and other biological factors in the development of social phobia presents an exciting challenge for future research. Technological advances, such as brain imaging devices, used to measure neurological activity in people with other kinds of anxiety, have only begun to be used to study people with social anxiety. Future technology might help determine what parts of the brain are activated when someone experiences the fear of disapproval.

Future studies may help us understand one biological aspect of social phobia; epidemiologists and geneticists will need to study another—the possibility that social phobias run in families. This is a complicated issue. The biggest difficulty is in determining why some families experience more than their share of social phobias. Is it because they have the same genes, or because they share the same environment? Some laboratory researchers hope to find the answer by discovering a gene that may, in part, be responsible for social phobias. Other researchers are studying the families of people with social phobias. Twin studies are one particularly important type of family research addressing the questions of heredity versus environment. Twins from the same egg (monozygotic) can be compared to twins from different eggs (dizygotic), and twins raised apart can be compared to twins raised in the same household. This type of research will be instrumental in determining which aspects of social phobias are inherited and which are learned. As you might imagine, this type of research is extremely time-consuming and very expensive. However, until such studies can be conducted, our beliefs about the role of heredity and environment in the development of social phobias will be based on limited information.

We have much to learn about how a person's environment influences social phobias. It has long been believed that certain early childhood experiences determine whether social phobias develop in adulthood. For example, some research has found that children who have a school phobia are more likely to develop a social phobia when they grow up. However, such retrospective research has been based on the childhood memories of adults; and such memories are often inaccurate. What is now needed is prospective research in which children with phobias are followed over the years to see if they later develop a social phobia. This type of longitudinal research can be used to study other aspects of an individual's environment that might affect social phobias. Other factors which might be important to study are the characteristics of parents and other family members, the kinds of information or misinformation individuals receive, and various life experiences they encounter growing up.

Even more important than studying biological or environmental factors alone is research that attempts to understand how these two types of factors interact. As you know from earlier chapters, we don't believe that one single cause of social phobia exists. It's much more likely that a number of things combine to increase your risk for having a social phobia. The challenge for scientists and theoreticians will be to develop explanations about the various ways in which risk factors, both biological and psychological, combine to cause a social phobia in a particular individual.

Do We Need To Know More about How To Recover?

Learning more about what causes a problem is important, in part, because it often provides clues about how to recover. If you've already overcome your social phobia, you may be wondering why more information is necessary. There are several reasons. First, some people have tried but are still unable to recover. Research is needed to discover why these people do not overcome their problem, and how existing treatments might be improved to help them join the ranks of those who are no longer disabled by the fear of disapproval.

Second, even when effective, current treatments almost always have side effects. Your medication may make you feel drowsy or produce other unpleasant symptoms. This is because no drug at present is able to target anxiety without affecting other aspects of the body and mind. Behavior therapy may have few physical side effects, but it can be uncomfortable and often raises your anxiety temporarily. (Wouldn't it be a relief to have a therapy with no side effects?) Third, effective treatments take time. Future research might discover ways to make these therapies work more rapidly.

Finally, because no two social phobias are exactly the same, it is not likely that one single technique will be found to be effective in all cases. Everyone's experience with fear of disapproval is different. Unless scientists discover a miracle cure that always works for everyone, the ultimate goal of future research should be to determine for each individual exactly which treatment will have the maximum effect with the least amount of effort and risk.

Can Social Phobias Be Prevented?

If science or society could prevent social phobias from developing in the first place, treatment advances wouldn't be necessary. Once again, a better understanding of what originally causes social phobias will be crucial to developing effective prevention programs. At the present time, we can only speculate about what such programs might involve. Some prevention efforts could be aimed at society in general. For example, educational programs could be instituted in grade schools across the nation. A more cost-effective approach might be to limit prevention programs to children who are at high risk for developing a social phobia. If such children can someday be identified ahead of time, it would then be feasible to institute more elaborate prevention strategies with this smaller segment of the population. We can safely predict that it will be some time before any kind of large-scale prevention program is implemented.

A Word in Closing

There are many unanswered questions about social phobia. Are human beings predisposed to develop social phobias? Have people always dreaded criticism, or are social fears the product of civilization? Is this a primary human fear, or did it evolve from the fear of physical harm? Are social phobias more prevalent in Western culture than in other societies? Do the media play a role in perpetuating social phobias? Why do fears of disapproval make people perform in ways that increase the chances of experiencing disapproval? And why do embarrassing responses like blushing, sweating, and shaking occur when people are socially anxious, but not necessarily when they experience other kinds of anxiety? These are intriguing questions. Their answers will reveal more than just the nature of social phobias. They will teach us something more about the nature of being human.

In the meantime, individuals with social phobia have every reason to be hopeful. The vast majority of the people we've worked with have made significant and oftentimes dramatic strides in overcoming their social fears. We've seen people who never thought they would work again recover from their phobia and go on to have exciting careers. We've also seen clients who were terrified at the mere thought of talking to others go on to have satisfying, long-term relationships. This new-found ability to participate in the social realm has made life for these people more fulfilling than they ever dreamed possible. We hope that by following the methods outlined in this book, either alone or with the aid of a mental health professional, you too will join the ranks of those who have battled their social fears and won.

References

Agras, W.S. (1990) "The treatment of social phobia." *Journal of Clinical Psychiatry* 51 (suppl.): 52-55.

Aimes, P., M. Gelder, and P. Shaw (1983) "Social phobia: A comparative clinical study." *British Journal of Psychiatry* 142: 14-179.

Barlow, D.H (1988) *Anxiety and Its Disorders: The Nature of Treatment of Anxiety and Panic.* New York: Guilford Press.

Barlow, D.H., P.A. DiNardo, B.B. Vermilyea, J.A. Vermilyea, and E.B. Blanchard (1986) "Comorbidity and depression among the anxiety disorders: Issues in diagnosis and classification." *Journal of Nervous and Mental Disease* 174: 63-72.

Barr Taylor, C., and B. Arnow (1988) *The Nature and Treatment of Anxiety Disorders.* New York: International Universities Press.

Beck, A.T. (1976) *Cognitive Therapy and the Emotional Disorders.* New York: International Universities Press.

Beck, A.T., G. Emery, and R. Greenberg (1985) *Anxiety Disorders and Phobia: A Cognitive Perspective.* New York: Guilford Press.

Bernstein, D.A., and T.D. Borkovec (1973) *Progressive Relaxation Training: A Manual for the Helping Professionals.* Champaign, IL: Research Press.

Burns, D. (1980) *Feeling Good: The New Mood Therapy.* New York: William Morrow & Company.

_____. (1989) *The Feeling Good Handbook.* New York: William Morrow & Company.

Davidson, J.R.T., S.M. Ford, R.D. Smith, and N.L.S. Potts (1991) "Long-term treatment of social phobia with clonazepam." *Journal of Clinical Psychiatry* 52 (suppl): 16-20.

deSilva, P., and S. Rachman (1981) "Is exposure a necessary condition for fear reduction?" *Behavior Research and Therapy* 19: 227-232.

Ellis, A. (1970) *The Essence of Rational Psychotherapy: A Comprehensive Approach to Treatment.* New York: Institute for Rational Living.

Hall, E.T. (1963) "A system for the notation of proxemic behavior." *American Anthropologist* 65: 1003-1026.

Heimberg, R.G., R.E. Becker, K. Goldfinger, and J. Vermilyea (1985) "Treatment of social phobia by exposure, cognitive restructuring and homework assignments." *Journal of Nervous and Mental Disease* 173: 236-245.

Heimberg, R.G., C.S. Dodge, and R.E. Becker (1987) "Social phobia." In *Anxiety and Stress Disorders*, edited by L. Michelson, and M.L. Ascher. New York: Guilford Press.

Heimberg, R.G., and D.H. Barlow (1991) "New developments in cognitive-behavioral therapy for social phobia." *Journal of Clinical Psychiatry* 52 (suppl.): 21-30.

Hollis, J. (1985) *Relapse for Eating Disorder Sufferers*. Center City, MN: Hazelden Educational Materials.

Lanzetta, J.T., J. Cartwright-Smith, and R.E. Kleck (1976) "Effects of nonverbal dissimulations on emotional experience and autonomic arousal." *Journal of Personality and Social Psychology* 33: 354-370.

Liebowitz, M.R. (1987) "Social phobia." *Modern Problems in Pharmaco-psychiatry* 22: 141-173.

Liebowitz, M.R., J.M. Gorman, A.J. Fyer, and D.F. Klein (1985) "Social phobia: Review of a neglected anxiety disorder." *Archives of General Psychiatry* 42: 729-736.

Liebowitz, M.R., J.M. Gorman, A.J. Fyer, et al. (1988) "Pharmacotherapy of social phobia: An interim report of a placebo-controlled comparison of phenelzine and atenolol." *Journal of Clinical Psychiatry* 49: 252-257.

Liebowitz, M.R., F.R. Schneier, E. Hollander, L.A. Welkowitz, J.B. Asoud, J.F. Campeas, B.A. Fallon, L. Street, and A. Gitow (1991) "Treatment of social phobia with drugs other than benzodiazepines." *Journal of Clinical Psychiatry* 52 (suppl.): 10-15.

Mahoney, M.J. (1974) *Cognitive and Behavior Modification*. Cambridge, MA: Ballinger.

Matthews, A.M., M.G. Gelder, and D.W. Johnston (1981) *Agoraphobia: Nature and Treatment*. London: Tavistock Publications.

Mattick, R.P., and L. Peters (1988) "Treatment of severe social phobia: Effects of guided exposure with and without cognitive restructuring." *Journal of Clinical and Consulting Psychology* 56: 251-260.

McGlynn T.J., and H.L. Metcalf (1989) *Diagnosis and Treatment of Anxiety Disorders: A Physician's Handbook*. Washington, D.C.: American Psychiatric Press.

Meichenbaum, D. (1974) *Cognitive Behavior Modification.* Morristown, N.J.: General Learning Press.

Ohman, A. (1986) "Face the beast and fear the face: Animal and social fears as prototypes for evolutionary analyses of emotion." *Psychophysiology* 23: 123-145.

Ohman, A., G. Erixon, and I. Lofburg (1975) "Phobias and preparedness: Phobic versus neutral pictures as conditional stimuli for human autonomic responses." *Journal of Abnormal Psychology* 84: 41-45.

Ohman, A., U. Dimberg, and L.G. Ost (1985) "Animal and social phobias: A laboratory model." In *Trends in Behavior Therapy,* edited by P.O. Sjoden, and S. Bates. New York: Academic Press.

Rosenbaum, J. (1990) "Overview of benefit/risk issues in clinical practice." Paper presented at the Panic Awareness for the Clinician Conference, at Carlsbad, CA.

Schneier, F.R., L.Y. Martin, M.R. Liebowitz, J.M. Gorman, and A.J. Fyer (1989) "Alcohol abuse in social phobia." *Journal of Anxiety Disorders* 3: 15-23.

Sheehan, D. (1983) *The Anxiety Disease.* New York: Charles Scribner's Sons.

Stein, M.B., M.E. Tancer, C.S. Gelernter, B.J. Vittone, and T.W. Uhde (1990) "Major depression in patients with social phobia." *American Journal of Psychiatry* 147: 637-639.

Torgerson, S. (1983) "Genetic factors in anxiety disorders." *Archives of General Psychiatry* 40: 1085-1089.

Zuckerman, M., R. Klorman, D.T. Larrance, and N.H. Spiegel (1981) "Facial, autonomic, and subjective components of emotion: The facial feedback hypothesis versus the externalizer-internalizer distinction." *Journal of Personality and Social Psychology* 41: 929-944.

Barbara G. Markway, Ph.D., is a clinical psychologist in private practice in St. Louis, Missouri. She completed a postdoctoral fellowship in the Anxiety Disorders Center at St. Louis University Medical Center, where she specialized in the cognitive-behavioral treatment of social phobia and other anxiety disorders.

Cheryl C. Carmin, Ph.D., is an assistant professor of psychiatry and human behavior and the assistant director of the Anxiety Disorders Center at St. Louis University Medical Center. She completed a postdoctoral fellowship at Case Western Reserve University School of Medicine and University Hospitals of Cleveland, where she specialized in the treatment of anxiety disorders.

C. Alec Pollard, Ph.D., is an associate professor of psychiatry and human behavior and the director of the Anxiety Disorders Center and the Behavioral Treatment Unit at St. Louis University Medical Center. His research in the area of anxiety disorders is widely-published. He is an advisor to the DSM-IV Social Phobia Work Group.

Teresa M. Flynn, Ph.D., currently works as a psychologist in the Anxiety Disorders Center at St. Louis University Medical Center. Her training included a postdoctoral fellowship in behavioral medicine at St. Louis University Medical Center.

Some Other New Harbinger Self-Help Titles

Virtual Addiction, $12.95
After the Breakup, $13.95
Why Can't I Be the Parent I Want to Be?, $12.95
The Secret Message of Shame, $13.95
The OCD Workbook, $18.95
Tapping Your Inner Strength, $13.95
Binge No More, $14.95
When to Forgive, $12.95
Practical Dreaming, $12.95
Healthy Baby, Toxic World, $15.95
Making Hope Happen, $14.95
I'll Take Care of You, $12.95
Survivor Guilt, $14.95
Children Changed by Trauma, $13.95
Understanding Your Child's Sexual Behavior, $12.95
The Self-Esteem Companion, $10.95
The Gay and Lesbian Self-Esteem Book, $13.95
Making the Big Move, $13.95
How to Survive and Thrive in an Empty Nest, $13.95
Living Well with a Hidden Disability, $15.95
Overcoming Repetitive Motion Injuries the Rossiter Way, $15.95
What to Tell the Kids About Your Divorce, $13.95
The Divorce Book, Second Edition, $15.95
Claiming Your Creative Self: True Stories from the Everyday Lives of Women, $15.95
Six Keys to Creating the Life You Desire, $19.95
Taking Control of TMJ, $13.95
What You Need to Know About Alzheimer's, $15.95
Winning Against Relapse: A Workbook of Action Plans for Recurring Health and Emotional Problems, $14.95
Facing 30: Women Talk About Constructing a Real Life and Other Scary Rites of Passage, $12.95
The Worry Control Workbook, $15.95
Wanting What You Have: A Self-Discovery Workbook, $18.95
When Perfect Isn't Good Enough: Strategies for Coping with Perfectionism, $13.95
Earning Your Own Respect: A Handbook of Personal Responsibility, $12.95
High on Stress: A Woman's Guide to Optimizing the Stress in Her Life, $13.95
Infidelity: A Survival Guide, $13.95
Stop Walking on Eggshells, $14.95
Consumer's Guide to Psychiatric Drugs, $16.95
The Fibromyalgia Advocate: Getting the Support You Need to Cope with Fibromyalgia and Myofascial Pain, $18.95
Healing Fear: New Approaches to Overcoming Anxiety, $16.95
Working Anger: Preventing and Resolving Conflict on the Job, $12.95
Sex Smart: How Your Childhood Shaped Your Sexual Life and What to Do About It, $14.95
You Can Free Yourself From Alcohol & Drugs, $13.95
Amongst Ourselves: A Self-Help Guide to Living with Dissociative Identity Disorder, $14.95
Healthy Living with Diabetes, $13.95
Dr. Carl Robinson's Basic Baby Care, $10.95
Better Boundaries: Owning and Treasuring Your Life, $13.95
Goodbye Good Girl, $12.95
Fibromyalgia & Chronic Myofascial Pain Syndrome, $19.95
The Depression Workbook: Living With Depression and Manic Depression, $17.95
Self-Esteem, Second Edition, $13.95
Angry All the Time: An Emergency Guide to Anger Control, $12.95
When Anger Hurts, $13.95
Perimenopause, $16.95
The Relaxation & Stress Reduction Workbook, Fourth Edition, $17.95
The Anxiety & Phobia Workbook, Second Edition, $18.95
I Can't Get Over It, A Handbook for Trauma Survivors, Second Edition, $16.95
Messages: The Communication Skills Workbook, Second Edition, $15.95
Thoughts & Feelings, Second Edition, $18.95
Depression: How It Happens, How It's Healed, $14.95
The Deadly Diet, Second Edition, $14.95
The Power of Two, $15.95
Living Without Depression & Manic Depression: A Workbook for Maintaining Mood Stability, $18.95
Couple Skills: Making Your Relationship Work, $14.95
Hypnosis for Change: A Manual of Proven Techniques, Third Edition, $15.95
Letting Go of Anger: The 10 Most Common Anger Styles and What to Do About Them, $12.95
Infidelity: A Survival Guide, $13.95
When Anger Hurts Your Kids, $12.95
Don't Take It Personally, $12.95
The Addiction Workbook, $17.95

Call **toll free, 1-800-748-6273**, or log on to our online bookstore at **www.newharbinger.com** to order. Have your Visa or Mastercard number ready. Or send a check for the titles you want to New Harbinger Publications, Inc., 5674 Shattuck Ave., Oakland, CA 94609. Include $3.80 for the first book and 75¢ for each additional book, to cover shipping and handling. (California residents please include appropriate sales tax.) Allow two to five weeks for delivery.

Prices subject to change without notice.